D0001558

DARWIN'S ENIGMA:
Fossils and Other Problems

By
Luther D. Sunderland

MASTER BOOK PUBLISHERS
SANTEE, CALIFORNIA
92071

575
Au 72

DARWIN'S ENIGMA

Copyright © 1984 Luther D. Sunderland
3rd Edition

Published by
Master Book Division of CLP
P.O. Box 1606
El Cajon, California 92022

Library of Congress Catalog Card Number 84-062231
ISBN 0-89051-108-X

Cataloging in Publication Data

Sunderland, Luther D., 1929-
    Darwin's Enigma: Fossils and Other Problems
    1. Evolution 2. Paleontology 3. Science

    I. Title

QH 365.02   1984   575   84-62231
ISBN 0-89051-108-X

88.3 - 98

Cover by Colonnade Graphics, El Cajon, CA

Printed in the United States of America

"Promoting neither the creationist nor the evolutionist position, Luther Sunderland has extensively researched the origins of man. This new book presents his unusual findings in an unconventional approach certain to shake up both traditional camps — and to delight the inquisitive student."

Theodore M. Black
Chancellor Emeritus
New York State Board of Regents

"Open academic inquiry in the teaching of theories on origins is a basic tenet of a free society. Scientific evidences relating to the origin of life should be presented without bias in its alternative forms. Mr. Sunderland takes a provocative and stimulating look at the scientific evidences on origins, emphasizing the fossil evidence, to let the reader be better informed on the subject."

Prof. Robert L. Frantz
Head, Dept. of Mineral Engineering
Pennsylvania State University

"Previous texts relative to the creation-evolution controversy have attempted to cover too much ground. That has been avoided here. Mr. Sunderland has done an excellent job of amassing critical opinion from the scientific community relative to fossil evidence which is, of course, the historical narrative of life on earth.

Scientists and non-scientists alike should find it interesting to confront the difficult questions asked. I certainly will encourage my students and colleagues to read this valuable treatise."

Robert Jenkins
Professor of Biology
Ithaca College

Table of Contents

Preface

Scientific research demands that the results of its investigatory process be verifiable through repeated testing. Dramatic advances in such sciences as medicine, space, and computers are verifiably evident in our increased life span, in our pinpoint landing on the moon, and in the unerring accuracy of the electronic computer.

Researchers in the field of evolution, however, have produced no verifiable facts that would validate their theory conclusively. From time to time evolutionists have even admitted ignoring real facts and altering the theory to fit selected data. In spite of these grossly unscientific tactics, the theory of evolution continues to be presented in textbooks, encyclopedias, and research papers as if it were a proven and verifiable scientific fact.

The author of *Darwin's Enigma: Fossils and Other Problems* has focused the spotlight of truth on the theory of evolution, showing that the dramatic fossil evidence indicates that all life did *not* have a common ancestor!

There remains only the trust that those with a vested interest in the theory of evolution as currently presented in textbooks will permit an equal opportunity for all students to be exposed to all scientific evidences and to the only competitive theory of origins. Some local school boards, state school boards, scientists, and parents will be distressed at the imagined implication of "religion" in our public schools. But the theory that life abruptly appeared on Earth is no more a religious absolute than the theory of evolution, for they are both axioms and neither is subject to scientific proof.

The time has come for the powers-that-be to recognize that our students at all grade levels are entitled to know both sides of the creation/evolution controversy. Luther Sunderland's book, *Darwin's Enigma: Fossils and Other Problems*, presents the facts from both a present day and historical perspective. This is *must* reading for all students, teachers and scientists.

Genevieve S. Klein, B.S., M.A., LL.D., L.H.D.
Regent Emerita, New York State Board of Regents

Chapter 1

The Problem Won't Go Away 100 Years After Darwin

There is a widespread and ever-escalating interest in the subject of origins, not only regarding the origin of the human race but how all life, the Earth and the universe came into existence. Mankind has always been curious about where things came from, but there has never been more concern about it than there is today.

With the mind-boggling advancement explosion in science and technology, solutions have been found for numerous problems and puzzles which for ages troubled the human race. Even in areas where complete solutions have not been realized, much encouraging progress has been made. Secrets of the atom have been unlocked and harnessed, worldwide transportation and communication have been made readily available to the public, the solar system has been explored, serious war has been avoided, many complex mysteries of the living cell unraveled and cures for diseases developed. But with each step of progress, the search for a scientific, naturalistic explanation for the origin of things has consistently and paradoxically been producing more questions than answers.

Hundreds of scientists who once taught their university students that the bottom line on origins had finally been figured out and settled are today confessing that they were completely wrong. They have discovered that their previous conclusions, once held so fervently, were based on very fragile evidences and suppositions which have since been refuted by new discoveries. This has necessitated a change in their basic philosophical position on origins. Others are admitting great weaknesses in evolution theory. One of the world's most highly respected philosophers of science, Dr. Karl Popper, has argued that one theory of origins, almost universally accepted as a scientific *fact*, does not even qualify as a scientific theory. A 1980 display at the prestigious British Museum of Natural History made the same admission.

Outer space was once believed to hold the key to unlocking the mystery of origins, but explorations of the moon, Mars, Venus, Jupiter and Saturn emphatically brought down those hopes with a resounding crash. Just a few years ago, prominent scientists were making bold assertions that the evolution of life was not only probable but inevitable on other solar system planetary bodies and that the study of that life would help solve the mystery of the origin of terrestrial life. Now, however, they are giving up, convinced there is no hope of ever finding extraterrestrial life in the solar system and only the remotest hope of finding life anywhere except here on Earth. The millions of dollars spent on radiotelescopes in search of intelligent radio messages from outer space have produced only negative results.

When Watson and Crick discovered the helical structure of the DNA molecule and the general way that it coded the formation and replication of proteins in cells, there were great expectations that a plausible scientific explanation for the origin of life was just over the horizon. The laboratory synthesis of amino acids from basic chemicals further heightened the expectations that man, with all his intelligence and resources, could synthesize a living cell. These hopes have also been dashed with the failure to generate life in the laboratory, and researchers are stating that new natural laws will need to be discovered to explain how the high degree of order and specificity of even a single cell could be generated by random, natural processes.

Geology and paleontology held great expectations for

Charles Darwin, although in 1859 he admitted that they presented the strongest single evidence against his theory. Fossils were a perplexing puzzlement to him because they did not reveal any evidence of a gradual and continuous evolution of life from a common ancestor, proof which he needed to support his theory. Although fossils were an enigma to Darwin, he ignored the problem and found comfort in the faith that future explorations would reverse the situation and ultimately prove his theory correct. He stated in his book, *The Origin of Species*, "The geological record is extremely imperfect and this fact will to a large extent explain why we do not find intermediate varieties, connecting together all the extinct and existing forms of life by the finest graduated steps. He who rejects these views on the nature of the geological record, will rightly reject my whole theory."[1]

Now, after over 120 years of the most extensive and painstaking geological exploration of every continent and ocean bottom, the picture is infinitely more vivid and complete than it was in 1859. Formations have been discovered containing hundreds of billions of fossils and our museums now are filled with over 100 million fossils of 250,000 different species. The availability of this profusion of hard scientific data should permit objective investigators to determine if Darwin was on the right track.

What is the picture that the fossils have given us? Do they reveal a continuous progression connecting all organisms to a common ancestor? With every geological formation explored and every fossil classified it has become apparent that these, the only direct scientific evidences relating to the history of life, still do not provide any evidence for which Darwin so fervently longed. The gaps between major groups of organisms have been growing even wider and more undeniable. They can no longer be ignored or rationalized away with appeals to the imperfection of the fossil record. But those unwilling to accept defeat have altered the scenario a bit.

By the 1970s, prominent scientists in the world's greatest fossil museums were coming to grips with the so-called "gaps" in the fossil record and were cautiously beginning to present new theories of evolution that might explain the severe

conflicts between neo-Darwinian theory and the hard facts
of paleontology. Back in 1940, Dr. Richard B. Goldschmidt
had faced the horns of this dilemma-of-the-gaps with his
hopeful monster theory, the idea that every once in awhile
an offspring was produced that was a monster grossly different
from its parents.[2] Goldschmidt's revolutionary ideas were
ridiculed for many years but, by 1977, respected scientific
periodicals like the American Museum's *Natural History*
magazine were publishing articles predicting the vindication
of Goldschmidt's theory within a decade.[3] Dr. Niles
Eldredge, curator of Invertebrate Paleontology at the
American Museum, was collaborating with Dr. Stephen Jay
Gould of Harvard and calling their new theory, aimed at explaining the gaps, "punctuated equilibria." They thought
that it was an improvement over Goldschmidt's hopeful
monster theory, although it differed insignificantly.

Dr. David Pilbeam, curator of the Peabody Museum of
Natural History at Yale and later professor of anthropology
at Harvard, wrote an article in 1978 entitled "Rearranging
Our Family Tree" in which he stated that we had been wrong
in the past and that he was convinced we would not hit upon
the true or correct story of human evolution.[4]

Dr. David Raup, curator of geology at the Field Museum
of Natural History in Chicago, published an article in the
January 1979 issue of the museum's journal entitled "Conflicts Between Darwinism and Paleontology" in which he
stated that the 250,000 species of plants and animals recorded
and deposited in museums throughout the world did not
support the gradual unfolding hoped for by Darwin.[5] The
following April, Dr. Colin Patterson, a senior paleontologist
and editor of a prestigious journal at the British Museum of
Natural History, wrote in a letter to the author that he didn't
know of any real evidence of evolutionary transitions either
among living or fossilized organisms.[6]

By the late 1970s, debates on university campuses throughout the free world were being held on the subject of origins
with increasing frequency. Hundreds of scientists, who once
accepted the theory of evolution as fact, were abandoning ship
and claiming that the scientific evidence was in total support

of the theory of creation. Well-known evolutionists, such as Isaac Asimov and Stephen Jay Gould, were stating that, since the creationist scientists had won all of the more than one-hundred debates, the evolutionists should not debate them.

In December of 1978, the New York State Board of Regents directed the New York State Education Department to do a detailed study of how theories on origins should be treated in a revised version of the state's Regents Biology Syllabus. As part of their study, they invited the author to supply pertinent scientific information to the Bureau of Science Education which was conducting the study.

During the next year, the author conducted taped interviews with officials in five natural history museums containing some of the largest fossil collections in the world. The interviews were with Dr. Colin Patterson in London; Dr. Niles Eldredge in New York City; Dr. David M. Raup in Chicago; Dr. David Pilbeam in Boston; and Dr. Donald Fisher, state paleontologist at the New York State natural history museum. Written transcripts of the interviews were given to the New York State Education Department for use in their study on origins.

In these interviews, the paleontologists were questioned in detail about the nature of the fossil record from the deepest deposits containing fossils to the most recent. Typed transcripts of the five interviews were then sent to the interviewees for editing. All but Dr. Patterson made editorial corrections before they were published for use by educators in various states.

This book presents the substance of these interviews through the use of short excerpts and summaries of the replies to the questions. Anyone, however, can gain access to the original typed verbatim interview transcripts which were prepared for the New York State Education Department by going to any public libarary in the United States and asking for the ERIC Document Reproduction Service microfiche ED 228 056, *Darwin's Enigma: The Fossil Record.*

If information about the true nature of the fossil record, so vividly described in these interviews, were to be presented without bias in public school textbooks, there would be no need for over half of the state legislatures to be considering legislation requiring open academic inquiry into the teaching of theories on origins. It is not so much a problem of failing to include in textbooks the simple factual statement that there is an alternative to evolution theory—which is accepted by the majority of the public — that a Supernatural Power created the universe and first life. Rather, the main issue is that textbooks and other school materials are completely devoid of certain very significant scientific information which is talked about behind closed doors but not made available to the public. Should the information presented in this book be openly discussed in public education, the controversy would be defused and cease to be the hottest issue in public education.

Chapter 2

Darwinism and Science

Charles Darwin originated nothing really new in his book *On the Origin of Species by Means of Natural Selection or the Preservation of Favoured Races in the Struggle for Life.* The theory that everything had evolved by some natural process rather than being created by a Supernatural Power had been around for many years. In fact, it was one of the very oldest religious concepts. Some of its tenets, like the eternalness of matter, were included in the Babylonian creation epic, the *Enuma elish*, written about a thousand years before the book of Genesis was penned. Evolutionary ideas can be traced through the philosophies of many ancient nations including the Chinese, Hindu, Egyptian, and Assyrian. The Egyptians for example had long believed in the spontaneous generation of frogs after the Nile had flooded, and the Chinese thought that insects appeared from nothing on the leaves of plants. The first to elucidate the theory of evolution in a clear, coherent manner, involving a simple-to-complex progression, was Thales of Miletus (640-546 B.C.) His was the first name to be mentioned in Greek science. He began with water which developed into other elements. These first elements developed into plants, then into simple animals, and finally into more complex forms like man.[1]

Evolutionary concepts were handed down through the Greek philosophers, such as Plato and his pupil, Aristotle, all the way to Darwin's grandfather, Erasmus Darwin (1731-1802). "Darwinism" was a term first applied to the evolutionary ideas of Erasmus Darwin, a well-known physician in England. His grandson, Charles, was quite familiar with the concepts of evolution that Erasmus Darwin and numerous others were discussing in the early 1800s.

As a well-known personality in England, Erasmus Darwin was an important pioneer and spokesman for the early evolutionists. In addition to serving as a prominent physician for nobility, he wrote philosophy and poetry. The two questions he asked about origins were: Did all living creatures, including man, descend from a single common ancestor and, if so, how could species be transformed from one to the other? In support of common-ancestry evolution, he assembled a surprisingly modern-sounding list of arguments based on embryology, classification, fossils, and geographical distribution. According to Richard Leakey and Roger Lewin in *Origins*, the question about a mechanism was "trickier to deal with," but Erasmus Darwin's treatment contained the seeds of almost all the important principles of modern evolutionary theory. He thought that overpopulation, competition—even between males and females—and selection were involved. He also believed that plants should not be left out of the evolutionary picture (as they virtually are today). He seemed to accept the possibility that the principal force in animal evolution was active adaptation to environment, including inheritance of acquired characteristics.[2]

Charles Darwin was born in 1809, seven years after his grandfather's death. Although he did not have the opportunity to discuss evolutionary ideas with his grandfather, he did read his book. According to Gertrude Himmelfarb in her biography *Darwin and the Darwinian Revolution*, Darwin relegated his grandfather Erasmus to a footnote in his "Historical Sketch" as having anticipated the views and erroneous grounds of opinion of Lamarck.[3] It does seem rather inexplicable that Darwin failed to give his grandfather any recognition for his contribution to the theory of evolution which he presented in *The Origin* as though it were an original idea.

A Frenchman, Jean Baptiste de Lamarck (1744-1829), pursued the idea that acquired characteristics could be passed on to offspring, as suggested by Erasmus Darwin. His most famous example was the neck of the giraffe, which was supposed to have resulted from stretching to reach higher and

higher vegetation as a drought dried up the lower leaves.
Lamarck brought considerable criticism upon the theory of
evolution. In 1813, three men independently presented rebut-
tals of Lamarckism at the Royal Society in London, and they
all supported the concept of natural selection. Regardless of
his own criticism of it, Darwin still occasionally yielded to
Lamarckism when writing his 1859 book, resorting to it to
explain the origin of the giraffe's long neck.

In *What Darwin Really Said*, historian Farrington recognized Darwin's lust for fame and thus his failure to acknowledge the previous contributions by others: "No reader,
however, could guess from the opening page of *The Origin*
that descent with modification had a long history before
Darwin took up his pen." He showed how Darwin pretended
to have just stumbled upon the idea while on the *Beagle* and
upon his return home. After talking about "that mystery of
mysteries," Darwin wrote, "After five years' work I allowed
myself to speculate on the subject." Not a word about his
grandfather Erasmus, Lamarck or any of the others, like
Matthew, who had written about the subject in 1831: "...
those only come to maturity (who have survived) the strict
ordeal by which nature tests their adaptation to her standards
of perfection and fitness to continue their kind by reproduction." Farrington notes, "The subject was in the air, and
Darwin does not say so."[4]

Evolutionists, however, did not have exclusive claim to the
concept of natural selection: one of the chief proponents of
creation, the only rival view, accepted it. Before Darwin, one
of the most popular books on origins was Paley's *Natural
Theology or Evidences of the Existence and Attributes of the
Deity collected from the Appearances of Nature* (1802).[5]
Historian Farrington wrote that Darwin was quite familiar
with Paley's book: "Darwin read him with delight and found
his logic as cogent as that of Euclid."[6] There can be no question
that Paley's arguments for natural selection were well known
to Darwin. As Gould noted in *Science* magazine, "Darwinians
cannot simply claim that natural selection operates since
everyone, including Paley and the natural theologians,
advocated selection as a device for removing unfit individuals

at both extremes and preserving, intact and forever, the
created types."[7] He said that all creationists accepted natural
selection and that Paley's book contained many references to
selective elimination.

Creationist Edward Blyth, in 1835 and 1837, wrote articles
for the *Magazine of Natural History* in which he proposed
the same idea that Darwin claimed to have thought of a year
later.[8] Blyth wrote regarding food gathering in animals,
". . . the one best organized must always obtain the greatest
quantity; and must, therefore, become physically the strongest
and be thus enabled, by routing its opponents, to transmit its
superior qualities to a greater number of its offspring."
Clearly, this is natural selection and survival of the fittest in
the purest sense. Darwin is known to have been familiar with
this magazine and so would have read Blyth's articles. Evolutionist Loren Eiseley has asserted that Darwin got the whole
idea from Blyth. Darwin's biographers puzzle over his failure
to give credit to others before him who wrote publicly about
evolution through natural selection. It *was* rather ungentle-
manly of him.

The creationist and evolutionist views on natural selection
differed in that creationists thought it was a conservative
principle while evolutionists saw it as a force that worked in
concert with random changes to create every living thing from
a common ancestor. Evolutionists claimed that natural selection took the randomness out of random variation and made
it a directional, creative force which drove certain living
organisms inexorably to higher levels of complexity.

The major contribution made by Charles Darwin when he
published his famous book in November 1859 was to open an
attractively packaged Pandora's box and release it to a waiting world. His book simply served to popularize an existing
idea which skeptics of the then widely accepted Genesis
account of creation welcomed with open arms.[9] Previously,
they had no single cohesive text that seemed to tie it all together and offer a possible mechanistic explanation for everything. *The Origin* attempted to explain the origination of the
great diversity of life without the necessity of any divine
power, as historian Gillespie emphasized in his 1979 book

Charles Darwin and the Problem of Creation.
Besides his lifelong wrestling with the question of religion and origins, Darwin was a man of many conflicts and inconsistencies. In the latter part of his school life he became passionately fond of shooting and he said, "I do not believe that anyone could have shown more zeal for the most holy cause than I did for shooting birds."[10] Yet he thought it was wrong to kill an insect and took to collecting those that he found already dead. In his *Autobiography* (1882) he wrote, "I almost made up my mind to begin collecting all the insects which I could find dead, for on consulting my sister, I concluded that it was not right to kill insects for the sake of making a collection."[11] He had a strong taste for fishing but could not stand putting a live worm on a hook. He explained, "I was told that I could kill the worms with salt and water, and from that day I never spitted a living worm, though at the expense, probably, of some loss of success...."[12] So the current idol of the biological world could not kill a fly or put a live worm on a hook, but he had the utmost zeal for shooting birds.

Darwin portrayed himself as a rather dull student, writing that school was "simply a blank. During my whole life I have been singularly incapable of mastering any language." He said that he "could never do well at verse making." Although he could learn forty or fifty lines of poetry while in morning chapel, he totally forgot them within two days. He wrote, "I believe that I was considered by all my masters (teachers) and by my father as a very ordinary boy, rather below the common standard in intellect."[13]

Charles Darwin's physician father wanted his son to follow in his footsteps, so he sent Charles to medical school at the University of Edinburgh. There Charles soon discovered that he did not have the stomach for such work. He thought that the lectures on anatomy were dull and the subject disgusted him. During his second year he attended lectures on geology and zoology, but said in his *Autobiography*, "they were incredibly dull. The sole effect they produced on me was the determination never as long as I lived to read a book on geology or in any way to study the science. Yet I feel sure I was prepared for a philosophical treatment of the subject...."[14] Although

Darwin's admirers contend (like Niles Eldredge did on a 1983 Boston television program) that Darwin was a geologist, he certainly never claimed to have formally studied the subject. He preferred only a "philosophical" treatment rather than a scientific study of geology. In his second year he dropped out of medical school. Since lack of money was not a problem for the Darwin family, he took up the more carefree pursuit of hunting game and collecting insects.

Not pleased to see Charles waste his life as "an idle sporting man," his father, although an atheist, decided that the lot of a country parson would be a more respectable profession, so he sent Charles off to divinity school at Cambridge University. Charles Darwin initially did believe in God and the Bible. In his *Autobiography* he wrote, "I did not then in the least doubt the strict and literal truth of every word in the Bible..."[15] but while at Cambridge he began questioning his faith. He wrote about his years there as follows: "During the three years which I spent at Cambridge my time was wasted, as far as the academical studies were concerned, as completely as at Edinburgh and at school. I attempted mathematics, and even went during the summer of 1828 with a private tutor (a very dull man) to Barmouth; but I got on very slowly. The work was repugnant to me, chiefly from my not being able to see any meaning in the early steps in algebra."[16] He said that Cambridge was worse than wasted because he got into a sporting set, including some "dissipated low-minded young men...we sometimes drank too much with jolly singing and playing cards afterwards."[17]

Nothing at Cambridge gave Darwin as much pleasure as collecting insects and he even got sketches of some of them published in a book. He concluded, "It seems therefore that a taste for collecting beetles is some indication of future success in life!"[18] Few historians would agree that it was his insect collecting that brought him fame. Rather it was being the first to publish a book that released the catch on a Pandora's box for a waiting world.

Darwin was quoted in the book *Life and Letters of Charles Darwin* as writing, "I gradually came to disbelieve in Christianity as a divine revelation.... Thus disbelief crept over me at a very slow rate, but was at last complete. The rate was so slow that I felt no distress."[19] Following graduation, two days after Christmas 1831, he set sail as a naturalist on board the British ship, *HMS Beagle*. During a five-year around-the-world voyage and shortly after his return to England, he came to accept the idea of the naturalistic, gradualistic origin of all species that his grandfather had promoted. Later he wrote, "But I had gradually come by this time, i.e. 1836 to 1839, to see that the Old Testament...was no more to be trusted than the sacred books of the Hindoos, or the beliefs of any barbarian..."[20]

By 1838 Darwin had adopted as an explanatory mechanism the "survival of the fittest" idea. Many of his admirers credit Charles Darwin with having originated the theory of evolution' by the mechanism of natural selection but, as already mentioned, he originated neither concept. Darwin admitted that natural selection was no more than the survival of the fittest idea which Herbert Spencer had described seven years before publication of *The Origin* in an 1852 pamphlet entitled "Theory of Population." Spencer wrote, "...those left behind to continue the race must be those in whom the power of self-preservation is the greatest—must be the select of their generation."[21] In another article that year, Spencer had expressed his firm belief in evolution which, through "insensible gradations" plus an infinity of time, could be supposed to produce man from a single-celled creature: "...surely if a single cell may, when subjected to certain influences, become a man in the space of twenty years, there is nothing absurd in the hypothesis that under certain other influences, a cell may, in the course of millions of years, give origin to the human race."[22]

Historian Bert Thompson contends that no person, other than perhaps geologist Charles Lyell, had as much influence on Darwin as Herbert Spencer.[23] Spencer was a prolific writer; he produced a ten-volume work on philosophy and many other books on topics such as biology, theory of population, and social statistics. Before he wrote on evolution, a dominant theme running through his writings was an abhorrence of anything supernatural. Speaking of his years between ages 18 and 20, he told how he slowly lost his religious beliefs:

Their hold had, indeed, never been very decided:
'The Creed of Christendom' being very evidently
alien to my nature, both emotional and intellectual."[24]

This antisupernatural bias was thus developed before
Spencer accepted the theory of evolution and it apparently
prepared the soil for the seed of this theory. Four years before
Darwin's *Origin of Species* was published, Spencer told why
he had adopted evolution:

Save for those who still adhere to the Hebrew
myth, or the doctrine of special creations derived
from it, there is no hypothesis but this hypothesis,
or (else) no hypothesis. The neutral state of having
no hypothesis can be completely preserved only
so long as the conflicting evidences appear exactly
balanced: such a state is one of unstable equilibrium,
which can hardly be permanent.

Spencer admitted that he adopted the evolutionary hypothesis for religious reasons in spite of scientific evidence against
it. He wrote, "For myself, finding that there is no positive
evidence of evolution...I adopt the hypothesis until better
instructed...." In addition to the "survival of the fittest" idea
which Darwin borrowed, Spencer had suggested many ideas
concerning evolution.

Another pre-Darwinian who must be given credit for his
contributions to the development of the evolutionary hypothesis is a Frenchman, Jean Baptiste de Lamarck, who died in
1829. He was a botanist and zoologist at a famous natural
history institution in Paris, now known as *Jardin des Plantes*.
Lamarck became one of the world's authorities on the classification of vertebrates. He was a brilliant scholar and a
committed evolutionist, according to Dr. Theodosius Dobz—
hansky, who wrote:

The first complete theory of evolution was that
of Lamarck (1809). It contained two elements. The
first and more familiar...is that organisms are
capable of changing their form, proportions, color,
agility, and industry in response to specific changes
in environment....Lamarck was the first modern

naturalist to discard the concept of fixed species,
and instead view species as variable populations.
He was the first to state explicitly that complex
organisms evolved from simpler ones.[25]

Lamarck proposed a tree of life, or phylogeny, based on the
assumption that every form of life came from a common
ancestor in a single evolutionary process. Evolutionist Ernst
Mayr of Harvard noted: "Stirrings of evolutionary thinking
preceded *The Origin* by more than 100 years, reaching an
earlier peak in Lamarck's *Philosophie Zoologique* in 1809."
It was in this book that Lamarck suggested the doctrine of
acquired characteristics for which he has become so famous.

Biographer Himmelfarb wrote that it was "indubitably true"
that the ideas Darwin presented in *The Origin* had already been
discussed and that "men's minds were prepared for it" before
Darwin first published his book.[26] It was thus no mere coin-
cidence that another naturalist, Alfred Russell Wallace,
should write a paper in 1858 which described virtually the
identical evolutionary hypothesis that Charles Darwin had
been discussing with close friends. When Darwin read
Wallace's paper, he quickly wrote one of his own and both
papers were read at the same meeting of the Linnean Society
in London in 1858 with Darwin and Wallace as coauthors. But
Darwin was destined to steal almost all of the limelight.

Darwin published a more definitive work the next year in
his well-known book *The Origin of Species*. Darwin's book
captured the imagination of a body of people with a particular philosophical bias who then rallied around it, unleas-
ing a force that gradually overcame almost all ideological opposition. In this respect, Darwin has had a more significant
impact on every facet of society throughout the world than
any other person in the last several hundred years. To some
degree, the theory of evolution has influenced the fields of
philosophy, economics, education, science, politics and, to
no minor degree, all major organized religious denomina-
tions, which now teach it exclusively in their seminaries,
either implicitly or explicitly.

Today, however, despite this tremendous record of success,
Darwinism is not faring well. In fact, some authors, like

Norman Macbeth, are claiming that it is actually dead and lacks only the final burial. But why is it in trouble after scoring such a sweeping victory? Simply because of its major weakness.

About twenty years ago some scientists discovered a serious problem with the theory of evolution and became very upset that they had been misled to think that it was as well established as the law of gravity. Consequently, an increasing number of scientists and others have been waging a campaign in public education to expose this major problem, as well as other flaws in the theory, and let the public in on what even some evolutionists admit has been a carefully guarded "trade secret."

The paradox is that the Achilles' heel of evolution theory turned out to be the very problem that troubled Darwin the most, namely, the lack of any fossil evidence to support the supposition that all life had come from a common ancestor. Indeed, although Darwin fervently hoped that further geological exploration would vindicate his theory, the fossil record has become "Darwin's enigma."

Only Two Theories on Origins

Often, in debates on origins theories, evolutionists assert that there could be many mechanistic theories of how living things originated. In his interview, however, Dr. Patterson said that he knew of only one theory besides gradualistic evolution— what Gould and Eldredge were calling "punctuated equilibria." He did not personally recognize "panspermia" (the idea that first life had been transported to Earth from outer space) as a satisfying solution because "that just puts the problem somewhere else." He said that if it did not start here on Earth it might have come by a fleet of rocketships, but he thought that really did not answer the question.

Dr. Raup said that, if there were a third possibility, it would be interplanetary seeding (panspermia) that should be considered. He agreed with Patterson that it did not really answer the question but just moved it back one planet. In a final exam some years ago, he had asked his students to disprove the proposition that trilobites (an extinct invertebrate) had arrived on Earth in a basket from outer space. He found much amusement in their squirming because, as he said, "It's difficult to disprove this." Panspermia was not, he thought, outside the sphere of scientific investigation for "One could look at the data and see if they are more compatible with that idea than any other."

This, incidentally, is not just a frivolous question with which a teacher can tease his students. It does not take a great amount of thought to see that evidence for the arrival of life from outer space in a basket and for the creation of complete life forms by God could be identical. In both cases, the first evidence of different types of life would show the abrupt appearance of complete functional organisms with no intermediates connecting them to anything basically different. So, if it is not outside the sphere of scientific investigation to evaluate the evidence for panspermia, it can hardly be claimed that the evidence for creation cannot be evaluated. If the fossil record showed the abrupt appearance of organisms without ancestors, that evidence would equally support either panspermia or creation.

Dr. Eldredge acknowledged that there were just the two concepts, namely, creation and evolution — the latter being explained by either Darwinism or his theory of punctuated equilibria. Later, he reiterated that there were "only two generally held views" on why we have diversity of life: evolution and creation. When asked if there could be a third, he said that there was a third biological one, spontaneous generation, but he thought that had "been abandoned" by biologists.

When it was noted, "But that doesn't differ from evolution which requires spontaneous generation of the first cell," Dr. Eldredge replied that he did not know. He said that it was in a sense, and then it was not, but there were currently just two theories in vogue. He viewed both as antithetical "sets of assumptions." He said that they were "axiomatic" in the sense that he did not "see one set falsifiable in favor of the other." He had discussed this with creationists and would not argue the point.

This is a major contention of perhaps all scientists who are creationists. They contend that no theory of origins can be tested completely and thus cannot be falsified. The reason is that evolution is supposed to be a one-time-only historical event or process that occurred in the past when there were no human observers, and it proceeded too rapidly in the past to have left any fossils. Evolutionists contend that today it is proceeding too slowly to be observed within the lifetime of any human observer. On the other hand, if various life forms abruptly appeared on Earth, whether by panspermia or creation, it would have been a unique historical event.

The museum officials seemed a bit uncertain about how to define a general theory of origins. Dr. Patterson thought there were three: Darwinian evolution, creation, and punctuated equilibria evolution. Dr. Raup also thought there were three: evolution, creation, and panspermia. Dr. Eldredge thought there were only two: evolution and creation. Other scientists say there are only two theories that are now seriously considered but, who knows, someone might think of another one someday.

This author likes to confine scientific discussions on the origin of life to theories that we can study here and now. It is possible, for example, to study the following questions scientifically: "How can we theorize that the great diversity of life on Earth might have originated and how can we evaluate these theories in the light of available scientific evidence?"

There are really only two general concepts as shown in Figure 1. Life either evolved from a common ancestor, or various different forms first appeared abruptly on Earth. The same three general explanations have been offered for both of these theories: purely mechanistic, theistic or unknown. The mechanistic explanation for evolution is either neo-Darwinism or punctuated equilibria; for abrupt appearance it is panspermia. The theistic explanation for evolution is called theistic evolution, and the theistic explanation for abrupt appearance is creation. The unknown possibilities are simply escape routes for those who do not wish to admit the obvious.

What Is Science?

Over the years, man has gradually systematized the quest for knowledge in order to separate good ideas from bad, fact

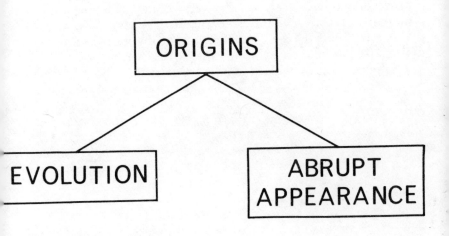

Figure 1. There are only two general concepts on origins. All ideas can be fitted into one of these.

from fantasy, and what we commonly call "science" from superstition. Actually, the original meaning of science was simply "knowledge." Science was a branch of the study of philosophy. Now it has come to be regarded as man's search for knowledge, in particular through the testing and falsification of ideas that have been devised to explain various natural phenomena, processes and facts that he has observed. Most people now think of science in the more narrow sense of "empirical science," or the branch of science that can be tested empirically in the laboratory, rather than simply knowledge or man's quest for knowledge. The systematic methodology scientists use in empirical science is called "the scientific method."

There are specialists who make their life's work out of developing and studying the systematic rules that have been found to be effective in the gaining of knowledge about the natural world. Their field is called the "philosophy of science." Roger Bacon in the 1200s and Francis Bacon in the 1600s are together given credit for originating the experimental method. In his *Novum Organum*, Francis Bacon established a new methodology for the experimental interpretation of nature.[27] It was Bacon's conviction that the mind, freed from the impediments of prejudices and generalizations, could, through knowledge, gain sovereignty over nature. He said that those who looked upon the laws of nature as something already explored and understood did philosophy and the sciences great harm. He criticized the Greeks for trusting too much in the force of their understanding and for making everything turn upon hard thinking and perpetual exercise of the mind. His method was based upon progressive stages of certainty. He stressed reduced dependence upon logic, which can have the effect of fixing errors rather than disclosing truth. Therefore, he proposed that the entire work of understanding be commenced afresh and that the mind not be left to take its own course but be guided at every step.

The essence of scientific experimentation is for man to be unshackled by preconceived ideas. Progress is to be made by experiment, discovery, and the establishment of fact by the observation of results.

The modern-day Francis Bacon is Professor Karl Popper, German-born philosopher of science now living in England. He has made great contributions to our understanding of science. Nobel Prize-winner Peter Medawar calls Popper "incomparably the greatest philosopher of science who has ever lived."[28] At a seminar held at Cambridge University to discuss Stephen Gould's ideas on evolution (30 April - 2 May 1984), Medawar summed up the meeting with the observation that no theory, no matter how well established, can be considered exempt from Popperian challenge.

Hermann Bondi has stated, "There is no more to science than its method, and there is no more to its method than Popper has said."[29]

Popper strongly supports the idea that a theory in science must be testable and, for the tests to be valid, they must be capable of falsifying the theory if it is not correct. It follows that a true scientific theory, in order to be tested, must be about a process that can be repeated and observed either directly or indirectly. One-time-only historical events may be true, but they are not part of science for there is no way of repeating them, observing them and subjecting them to testing. Also, for a theory to be testable, it must be possible for those conducting the tests to use it in making predictions about the outcome of the tests. If a theory is not suitable for use by scientists to make specific predictions, it is not a scientific theory. Many scientists agree with Karl Popper on the testability requirement for a scientific theory because, without testing, there can be no unimpassioned selection among available alternatives.

Is Darwinism Testable Science?

According to the generally accepted requirements of a theory in science, could Charles Darwin's theory qualify as a truly scientific theory? Dr. Patterson did not think so. In his book, *Evolution*, he wrote, "If we accept Popper's distinction between science and non-science, we must ask first whether the theory of evolution by natural selection is scientific or pseudo-scientific (metaphysical).... Taking the first part of the theory, that evolution has occurred, it says that the history of life is a single process of species-splitting and progression.

This process must be unique and unrepeatable, like the history of England. This part of the theory is therefore a historical theory, about unique events, and unique events are, by definition, not part of science, for they are unrepeatable and so not subject to test."[30]

Of course, what Dr. Patterson calls "the first part of the theory, that evolution has occurred" is the only question under consideration in an evaluation of the validity of the theories on origins. Is it true that all life evolved from a common ancestor or isn't it? He says that the theory that life evolved is "by definition, not part of science." The second part simply postulates a mechanism for evolution if it did occur — mutations and natural selection. No one denies that mutations occur or that natural selection acts as a preservative principle in nature, but since these concepts are not exclusive tenets of evolution theory, they do not help differentiate that theory from its competitor. The only question remaining to be resolved is whether random changes, with the best ones preserved, could create successively higher levels of complexity, resulting in the entire biosphere.

In his interview, Dr. Patterson said that he agreed with the statement that neither evolution nor creation qualified as a scientific theory since such theories could not be tested. He liked a quote from R.L. Wysong's book *The Creation/Evolution Controversy* that both ideas had to be accepted on faith. A quote of L.T. More's, corroborating Huxley's comments, was:

> The more one studies paleontology, the more certain one becomes that evolution is based on faith alone; exactly the same sort of faith which is necessary to have when one encounters the great mysteries of religion....The only alternative is the doctrine of special creation, which may be true, but is irrational.[31]

Dr. Patterson said, in referring to this quotation, "I agree."

In one of their audiovisual displays in 1980, the British Museum of Natural History included the statement that evolution was not a scientific theory in the sense that it could not be tested and refuted by experiment. This devastating characterization of evolution brought a flurry of criticism from the scientific establishment and the museum quickly removed it from the display. In any other circumstances the media would have raised the objection of "censorship," but in this case they looked the other way.

What does Karl Popper say about evolution theory? In his autobiography *Unended Quest* he writes:

> I have come to the conclusion that Darwinism is not a testable scientific theory, but a metaphysical research programme — a possible framework for testable scientific theories. It suggests the existence of a mechanism of adaptation and it allows us even to study in detail the mechanism at work. And it is the only theory so far which does all that.
>
> This is of course the reason why Darwinism has been almost universally accepted. Its theory of adaptation was the first nontheistic one that was convincing; and theism was worse than an open admission of failure, for it created the impression that an ultimate explanation had been reached.
>
> Now to the degree that Darwinism creates the same impression, it is not so very much better than the theistic view of adaptation: it is therefore important to show that Darwinism is not a scientific theory but metaphysical. But its value for science as a metaphysical research programme is very great, especially if it is admitted that it may be criticized and improved upon.[32]

Of course, Popper is not saying much for his favored theory of Darwinism because any wild conjecture "may be criticized and improved upon." This is quite an admission for one who ridicules belief in theism.

Beverly Halstead, writing in *New Scientist* magazine, 17 July 1980, commented on Popper's position:

> Despite these subtle distinctions, it is not difficult to envisage the enormous encouragement the creationists take from assertions from the BM(NH) (British Museum display) that the theory of evolution is not scientific.[33]

Dr. Halstead told the author that his article drew so much

attention to the museum display that it was removed from the museum, and that Popper felt compelled to make a public statement that would quiet the storm without reversing or negating his previous pronouncements about the requirements of a scientific theory. In the 21 August 1980 issue of *New Scientist,* Popper replied:

> Some people think that I have denied scientific character to the historical sciences, such as paleontology, or the history of the evolution of life on Earth; or the history of literature, or of technology, or of science.
>
> This is a mistake, and I here wish to affirm that these and other historical sciences have in my opinion scientific character: their hypotheses can in many cases be tested.
>
> It appears as if some people would think that the historical sciences are untestable because they describe unique events. However, the description of unique events can very often be tested by deriving from them testable predictions or retrodictions.[34]

These are reasonable statements. No one ever said that nothing in paleontology, the history of life on Earth, literature, technology or science, could be studied through empirical testing. Nor has anyone claimed that it was not possible to make testable predictions or retrodictions from postulated unique historical events.

For example, from the hypothesis that all life evolved from a common ancestor through an unbroken chain, it is possible to predict that paleontology would uncover evidence in the fossil record of a gradual progression from single cell to man. Likewise, from the hypothesis that life abruptly appeared on Earth in complete functional form, it can be predicted that, without exception, the fossil record should show the first appearance of new organs and structures completely formed, and there should be no transitional forms connecting the major different types of organisms such as protozoa and metazoa, invertebrates and vertebrates, fishes and amphibians, amphibians and reptiles, etc. These predictions can be tested scientifically — and they have been, repeatedly. Interestingly,

Gillespie indirectly admitted this when he wrote, "There were ways in which Darwin's theory could clearly have been falsified. He named some of them. The absence of transitional fossils, however, was not one of them."[35] In other words, since Gillespie is a believer in Darwinism, he doesn't think it would be right to test the theory against the only direct scientific evidence, the fossil record, for he knows that evolution would flunk the test.

Professor Popper was careful not to contradict his previous clearly written statements that said, "Darwinism is not a testable scientific theory, but a metaphysical research programme." Metaphysics is not science but rather something more closely associated with religion. His calling the activity "research" does not make it scientific for it is possible to research anything, even the most bizarre superstitions. With his generalization that "very often" testable predictions could be derived from unique events, he did not specifically say that evolution was a scientific theory.

Investigators can test some sub-theory predictions of a general theory, but this does not automatically establish the general theory as a completely testable concept. This can be readily understood by considering the general historical theory that first life came to Earth in a rocket ship. The sub-theory that a living organism could crawl out of a rocket ship can be tested, but this does not test whether or not a rocket ship actually brought life from outer space. Similarly, the evolution sub-theory that populations change slightly can be tested, but this does not prove that the general theory of common-ancestry evolution is true.

Many other prominent scientists who are evolutionists admit that evolution theory is not really science. For instance, in the introduction to the 1971 edition of Darwin's *Origin of Species*, Dr. L. Harrison Matthews made the amazingly frank admission that evolution was faith, not science:

> The fact of evolution is the backbone of biology, and biology is thus in the peculiar position of being a science founded on an unproved theory — is it then a science or faith? Belief in the theory of evolution is thus exactly parallel to belief in special

creation — both are concepts which believers know
to be true but neither, up to the present, has been
capable of proof.[36]

Dr. Matthews probably did not actually mean to infer that
there was actually such a thing as a "proved theory" since he
must have known that no theory in science is ever really proved
in the technical sense. Theories are only falsified through testing, or they pass the test without exception until people become tired of testing them. What he must have meant was that
evolution had not once passed the test of comparing its predictions with the fossil record.

As mentioned previously, Dr. Eldredge was emphatic in
his contention that evolution theory was nothing but a body
of axioms. He repeated, "We have a body of axioms — the
creationist has and the evolutionist has — for which I can't
think of a crucial test." The author pointed out that it was nice
to talk with someone who did not try to throw in a third—
theistic evolution — which says that every time a change in the
DNA code is needed, God steps in. A third time Dr. Eldredge
reiterated the point that neither evolution nor creation could
be falsified through testing: "Nonetheless, I can't think of
any experiments which I might set up that would reject one
theory in favor of the other." This is an extremely significant
statement from a prominent scientist who has been leading the
national anticreationist organization, which is waging a battle
to maintain the exclusive teaching of only one of these axioms
in public schools—evolution. He explained why he personally
had adopted the set of "assumptions" that says there is a
"natural process which is creative." He thought that, if he
adopted this set of assumptions, he could then make predictions that would allow him to investigate the history of life.
Instead of investigating the fossil record to determine which
set of assumptions more closely fitted the facts, he made a
prior assumption that he had the answer to begin with. He
noticed certain sets of resemblances in living organisms and
said that the master question was to explain them. He said,
"There are two explanations of course. God had a plan, or as
you get away further from a common ancestor you get more
modification, so you get a nested set. It seems to me you must

accept one or the other axiomatically.".

So there could be no possibility of his statement being misinterpreted, he emphasized over and over that either evolution or creation had to be accepted as an axiom for neither one could be tested scientifically. Several years later he would have these words come back to haunt him when he joined the national anticreationist organization and felt compelled to try to defend evolution theory as pure, testable science, arguing that creation theory was only an axiom.

Arthur Koestler wrote about the unscientific nature of Darwinism and said that the education system was not properly informing people about this:

> In the meantime, the educated public continues to believe that Darwin has provided all the relevant answers by the magic formula of random mutations plus natural selection — quite unaware of the fact that random mutations turned out to be irrelevant and natural selection a tautology.[37]

In a symposium at the Wistar Institute in Philadelphia, prominent English evolutionist Dr. C.H. Waddington made some very pointed criticisms of neo-Darwinism as being a vacuous tautology. In commenting on a paper by Murray Eden entitled, "Inadequacies of Neo-Darwinian Evolution as a Scientific Theory," Dr. Waddington said:

> I am a believer that some of the basic statements of neo-Darwinism are vacuous;...So the theory of neo-Darwinism is a theory of the evolution of the changing of the population in respect to leaving offspring and not in respect to anything else. Nothing else is mentioned in the mathematical theory of neo-Darwinism. It is smuggled in and everybody has in the back of his mind that the animals that leave the largest number of offspring are going to be those best adapted also for eating peculiar vegetation, or something of this sort; but this is not explicit in the theory. All that is explicit in the theory is that they will leave more offspring.
>
> There, you do come to what is, in effect, a vacuous statement: Natural selection is that some things

leave more offspring than others; and you ask, which leave more offspring than others; and it is those that leave more offspring; and there is nothing more to it than that.

The whole real guts of evolution — which is, how do you come to have horses and tigers, and things — is outside the mathematical theory.[38]

Norman Macbeth has written a book, *Darwin Retried: An Appeal to Reason*, in which he gave an especially perceptive critique of Darwinism. Noted philosopher of science Karl Popper reviewed this book and endorsed it, calling it "a really important contribution to the debate."[39] In a 1982 interview, Macbeth had much to say about the major problems with evolution theory and about natural selection being a tautology:[40]

First, I think, is natural selection. When you ask all the different evolutionists to identify the real heart of evolution, they'll often give you three or four points — adaption, the number of generations, mutations and recombination. They've got a list of things that are supposed to be factors, but natural selection is on all lists and is obviously the dominant theory of all evolutionary discussion. With some people, it is the whole thing, so if you knock over natural selection, the whole structure crumbles.

Was natural selection the mechanism for evolution? He replied that it was, along with variation:

Variation is there but it does not accumulate, although they assert always that it does accumulate. Then you extrapolate it for another couple of hundred percent of the problem and you're in. Extrapolation is a terrible sin, so they've little foundation. The variation is there. You can see it, of course, in all the forms of dog we've bred, but accumulation and extrapolation are certainly used in a big way by evolutionists.

But isn't natural selection just a weeding out process? Macbeth explained:

A good evolutionist says it creates because everybody admits that something is weeding out. We are
always culling, just the ordinary operation of an
animal's life culls out the really weak ones. A faithful Darwinist says it is creative. Here we have the
opposition between evolutionist authors....
Michael Ruse says it can create anything...largely
by slow small changes accumulating. Gould, when
you read him very carefully, does not discern that
it creates new forms; it can mend and tinker, but it
is not producing really big new things.

Gould says that it might tune things up a bit, right? Macbeth:

He doesn't go much further than that. This is why
he confesses bankruptcy on the macroevolution
problem which Ruse will not confess. Ruse sees no
problem at all in macroevolution but Gould, with
a much keener eye for the limitations of natural
selection, says we haven't got anything to answer
that. He pins his hope for the future on epigenesis
which is pure hope.... They think the leap forward
would have occurred in the embryological gestation
period instead of among mature specimens. To
some extent they are pursuing a pipe dream too,
hoping to find serious evidence of it.

He told why he wrote that natural selection was an exercise
in circular reasoning:

I argued it was a tautology in my book because
it seemed to go round in a circle. It was, in effect,
defining survival as due to fitness and fitness as due
to survival. I also found people like Waddington
saying it was a tautology. He said that at the Darwinian centennial in 1959 in Chicago. Nevertheless,
he said it was a wonderful idea that explained
everything. Professor Ronald H. Brady goes a
little more deeply into it in his long articles in
Systematic Zoology[41] and the *Biological Journal
of the Linnean Society*[42]....I will not attempt to
summarize Brady's view, but I think it destroys the
idea of natural selection and this is certainly the

opinion of many people at the American Museum of
Natural History. It shoots to pieces the whole
basis for the Synthetic Theory....Few would
challenge Brady, but not because they understand
and approve.

Did Macbeth think that natural selection could act to
preserve life on Earth? Reply:

I think the phrase is utterly empty. It doesn't
describe anything. The weaker people die, a lot of
stronger people die too, but not the same percentage. If you want to say that is natural selection,
maybe so, but that's just describing a process. That
process would presumably go on until the last
plant, animal and man died out.

There appears to be a recent practice in certain circles to
call evolution a "fact" and not allow any discussion of its
factual status; simply talk about mechanisms. How legitimate
is this? How can a theory become an established fact? Could
evolution be considered an established fact? Macbeth says
that if evolution is defined as simply change, it could be called
a fact since we all agree there is much change, but if you equate
evolution with Darwinism, it is far from being a fact.

What about the oft-heard contention of evolutionists that
it is not permissible for anyone to attack an existing theory
until he can offer a better one? Macbeth is a member of the
systematics group at the American Museum which meets
frequently to discuss evolution primarily as it relates to
taxonomy — the classification of organisms. He has lectured
to them about the fallacy in this argument:

In my lecture to this group, I pointed out that they
succumbed repeatedly to the idea that if you want
to criticize a theory you ought to offer something
better. This I regarded as complete error...it
doesn't hold water. There is no duty to put something better in its place....I called this the 'best-
in-field fallacy.'...If the others are all hopeless
failures like Lamarckism, orthogenesis, or — as
they used to think — the hopeful monsters, it doesn't
do Darwinism much credit to be a little better

than they are....They say this is the best theory,
therefore, it must be good.

Gregory Pesely is another author who contends that natural
selection is nothing but a tautology:

One of the most frequent objections against the
theory of natural selection is that it is a sophisticated
tautology. Most evolutionary biologists seem
unconcerned about the charge and only make a
token effort to explain the tautology away. The
remainder, such as Professors Waddington and
Simpson, will simply concede the fact. For them,
natural selection is a tautology which states a
heretofore unrecognized relation: The fittest —
defined as those who will leave the most offspring —
will leave the most offspring.

What is most unsettling is that some evolutionary
biologists have no qualms about proposing tautologies as explanations. One would immediately
reject any lexicographer who tried to define a word
by the same word, or a thinker who merely restated
his proposition, or any other instance of gross
redundancy; yet no one seems scandalized that
men of science should be satisfied with a major
principle which is no more than a tautology.[43]

So scientists who believe in evolution admit that their
belief is based, not on scientific examination of the theory,
but rather on faith alone. This does not discourage them from
calling evolution a "fact" in an obvious attempt to promote
their belief without being able to justify it scientifically.

It is generally recognized that the original version of a
theory might not be entirely correct but not necessarily false
in every respect either. Thus, it is permissible for scientists to
attempt to salvage a theory that has flunked a test by making
secondary modifications to the theory and trying to make it
fit new facts not previously considered. A theory loses credibility if it must be repeatedly modified over years of testing
or if it requires excuses being continually made for why its
predictions are not consistent with new discoveries of data.
It is not a propitious attribute for a theory to have required

numerous secondary modifications. Some evolutionists mis-
understand this and attempt to point to the continuous string
of modifications to evolution theory as a justification for
classifying it as the exclusive respectable scientific theory on
origins. They often make the strange claim that creation
theory could not be scientific because it fits the evidence so
perfectly that it never has required any modification. That
line of reasoning is like saying that the law of gravity is not
scientific since it fits the facts so perfectly that it never needs
modification.

Of course, as mentioned above, a theory is never proven
absolutely true even if it has not once flunked extensive
scientific testing. Its credibility increases until scientists
develop so much confidence in it that they stop testing it.
Such a highly respected theory is commonly called a "scientific
law," like the law of gravity.

Some people mistakenly think that only scientists with a
high level of academic accomplishment are entitled to originate scientific theories and that their motivations must meet
certain requirements. Actually, a theory can start out as
nothing more than a flat guess, a religious concept, or it could
be the result of conclusions drawn from a deep study of detailed scientific data. The motivation of the person deriving a
theory can be as uncommendable as the desire to win an argument
or get a pay raise. As philosopher of science, professor Neal C.
Gillespie, wrote in his book *Charles Darwin and the Problem
of Creation*, "The source of an idea is irrelevant, in the strict
logical sense, to its success in a scientific system or in any
other. The procedures of proof in any knowledge system are
logically independent of the circumstances of the origin of
the ideas involved."[44]

In striking down the Arkansas "Balanced Treatment Act"
in 1982, Judge Overton contended that the theory of creation
could not be part of science because he thought it could be
derived only from a religious document. This demonstrated
his ignorance of the process of science. That is akin to saying
that because evolution is the basis of the first two tenets of the
Humanist Manifesto (the statement of faith of a tax exempt
religious organization) then it could not be true or be part of

science. Indeed the manifesto, signed by a number of prominent evolutionists, does read:

> Tenet 1: Religious humanists regard the universe as
> self-existing and not created.
> Tenet 2: Humanism believes that man is a part of nature
> and that he has emerged as the result of a continuous
> process.

Using Judge Overton's kind of logic, one would be compelled to exclude evolution from science because many of the
original formulators and promoters of the theory such as
Herbert Spencer (an atheist), Charles Darwin (an agnostic) and
Thomas Huxley (an agnostic), had religious motivations. It is
undoubtedly true that these men first became anticreationists
and nontheists on religious grounds. But this has no bearing
on whether or not evolution might be the correct explanation
of origins or whether it meets the requirements of a scientific
theory. The resolution of those questions is a matter entirely
separate from the motivation issue.

In any case, before a theory is subjected to extensive testing
by others, it is technically termed a "hypothesis." The most
important qualification for a scientific theory is that it be
testable, and, naturally, it must never have flunked a valid
test in its most mature form. So the questions that proponents of evolution theory are obligated to answer are: Can
evolution theory be subjected to repeated valid tests, and, if
so, can it pass those tests?

If there is any test that evolution theory should pass, it
is an evaluation against the fossil evidence, even though, as
Karl Popper asserts, you cannot prove history scientifically.
Though evolution theory postulates that there has been an
unbroken succession of organisms connected to a common
ancestor, it would not absolutely prove the theory if some
evidences of that series were actually found in the fossil record.
But it would be difficult to deny that this would be over-
whelming evidence in support of the theory of evolution; its
credibility would be considerably elevated. Nearly everyone
agrees with that. However, some people peculiarly deny that it
would falsify the theory or even raise serious questions about
its credibility if no evidence of such a series of intermediate

forms were found after over a century of intensive searching.

A major reason that the theory of evolution is not a falsifiable scientific theory seems to be that it is so plastic it can explain anything and everything. For example, Dr. Raup thought that evolution theory was falsifiable but, when asked why it had not been falsified when no intermediate forms had been found in the fossil record, he explained that the theory had just been modified to fit the evidence: "Well, whether it's valid or not, it's still possible to rationalize the lack of intermediates — rationalize it by simply modifying the original Darwinian theory."

It was then pointed out to him: "In debates, people say, 'Sure, the original Darwinian theory has been falsified, but we'll come up with a new one as fast as you can disprove the old ones.'" He acknowledged that this was true: "I think that's true of any conventional wisdom."

The author replied, "But that's not science. You've got to have a theory which is subject to falsification, and if it's falsified, throw in the towel. Now if you want to come up with a new theory, OK. But after it has been changed a hundred times and it is still falsified, at some point someone ought to throw in the towel. Maybe you could say, 'We don't know,' but don't put it in the textbooks and say it has been proven as well as any fact of science." Dr. Raup replied, "Yes, I'm sure you've seen how slowly conventional wisdom dies and it really takes overkill."

But regardless of whether or not theories on origins are truly scientific theories, the fossil record should at least shed some light on the question: Did the present biosphere originate from a common ancestor or did various major groups of organisms first appear abruptly on Earth? To find the evidence relating to fossils, it is only reasonable to consult specialists in some of the world's greatest museums which collect, study, and display fossils. The following chapters are based primarily upon material derived from the author's interviews with the officials at five such museums, as well as from a survey of the scientific literature on geology, paleontology, biology, and related fields.

Chapter 3

The Fossil Record — Nonlife to Reptiles

Historical Geology

On January 6, 1981 a spokesman for the American Association for the Advancement of Science, then meeting in Toronto, made the following statement which was reported over CBS television and radio:

> One hundred million fossils identified and dated in the world's museums constitute one hundred million facts that prove evolution beyond any doubt whatever....

That is the type of statement that evolutionary apologists commonly make when they are speaking to the general public. They make it sound like a closed case with all the facts already in and the decision pronounced by the judge and jury. The picture is entirely different, however, when one speaks to museum officials behind closed doors or when evolutionists speak to their fellow professionals. Let us look at this more candid picture given by leading natural history museum officials and by the scientific literature to see if the actual fossil record is consistent with such impressive-sounding pronouncements.

First, to understand many of the terms used in the interviews, it is necessary for the reader to have some knowledge of what is termed "historical geology." The foundational concept used in this field of study is the so-called "geologic column." This is a hypothetical layered arrangement of rocks supposedly representing vast periods of Earth history. Figure 2 shows the general structure of the geologic column as it existed in 1983.

The rocks that contain significant fossil deposits are the most pertinent to a discussion on the origin of life. These are placed in the upper portion of the column and fall into three major divisions called "eras." The Paleozoic era stretches from the deepest rocks that contain indisputable multicelled organisms (Cambrian) through the fishes, amphibians and reptiles. The Mesozoic era is the age of reptiles including dinosaurs and birds; Cenozoic era rocks contain fossils of mammals.

The geologic column was established before 1840 by men in England and Scotland when most of the world had not yet been explored geologically. It was based primarily on the observation of rocks in those two countries, some in the Paris basin, some in New York State, and some in Russia. Rock formations have never actually been found anywhere in the world in the complete arrangement shown in the column. Neither has there been even a significant portion of the column found in one place. The Grand Canyon has only about half of the Paleozoic deposits, but is missing the remainder of the fossil-bearing column. Formulators of the column based it upon the assumption that the fossils in successive layers of rocks should show a progression from simple to complex. Regardless of what has been found through the exploration of all continents since then, the basic column has not changed because of the philosophical bias of those who influence the scientific organizations and publications. It is virtually the only major concept in science that has not changed over and over in the past century.

In originally formulating the column, its composers did not necessarily base it on the assumption of evolution because at that time, they apparently believed in creation. They just thought that God had created more and more complex organisms from time to time and they interpreted the Bible accordingly in support of this view. Later, some of the formulators of the column, like Charles Lyell, switched to full acceptance of the theory that all living organisms had evolved from a common ancestor. Now virtually all geologists have

CENOZOIC	QUATERNARY	2
	TERTIARY	65
MESOZOIC	CRETACEOUS	144
	JURASSIC	208
	TRIASSIC	245
PALEOZOIC	PERMIAN	286
	CARBONIFEROUS	360
	DEVONIAN	408
	SILURIAN	438
	ORDOVICIAN	505
	CAMBRIAN	570

GEOLOGIC COLUMN

Figure 2. The geologic column is a hypothetical arrangement of rocks originally formulated by creationists. It purports to show a progression of organisms from simple to complex.

adopted a belief in evolution, so they insist that the hypothetical geologic column must maintain complete agreement
with that interpretive framework regardless of the evidence.

Since 1840, there have been many rock formations discovered with fossils completely out of order according to the
geologic column—like Precambrian setting on dinosaur-age
Cretaceous—but these have been either explained away or
simply ignored. Regardless of these serious problems, the
question of the validity of the geologic column will not be
addressed here. Rather, the standard column will be used as
the basis for discussing the fossil evidence since all natural
history museums use it in the dating, classification and
study of fossils.

The important question to be addressed here is: What do
the paleontologists say about the actual fossil evidences
found in the rocks? Do the fossils reveal a gradual progressive
continuum connecting all species to a common ancestor or do
they show the abrupt appearance of the major different groups
of organisms? That crucial question must be answered if we
are going to shed light on the issue of origins.

Cambrian Explosion

The nature of the fossil record was beginning to become
known by the mid-1800s, and Charles Darwin was acutely
aware of the picture that was emerging. In *The Origin of
Species,* he even candidly discussed the problems with the
fossil evidence. For example, he wrote:

> There is another and allied difficulty which is
> much more serious. I allude to the manner in which
> species belonging to the main divisions of the
> animal kingdom suddenly appear in the lowest
> known fossiliferous rocks....[1]

He even acknowledged that some of those animals were
almost unchanged in living species. So he recognized what
others failed to admit until Niles Eldredge and Stephen Gould
became famous for writing about it in the early 1970s: the
sudden appearance of the major groups plus stasis, little or
no change until extinction or the present. Darwin wrote:

> The abrupt manner in which whole groups of

species appear in certain formations has been urged by several paleontologists...as a fatal objection to the belief of the transmutation of species. If numerous species, belonging to the same genera or families, have really started into life at once, that fact would be fatal to the theory of evolution through natural selection. For the development by this means of a group of forms all of which are (according to the theory) descended from some one progenitor, must have been an extremely slow process; and the progenitors must have lived long before their modified descendants.[2]

What picture do the fossils give that would cause a man who committed his whole career to promoting common-ancestry evolution to make such devastating admissions about his pet theory? Let us first look at the deepest layer of rocks that contains any significant fossil deposits.

Most of the museums classify the deepest rocks that contain fossils of multicelled organisms as Cambrian rocks. Dr. Preston Cloud, writing in *Geology* magazine in 1973, stated that not a single indisputable multicellular fossil had been found anywhere in the world in a rock supposedly older than Cambrian rocks.[3] But in the Cambrian rocks is found a multitude of highly complex creatures with no ancestors. These rocks contain fossils of trilobites, brachiopods, corals, worms, pelecypods (clams), and soft-bodied creatures like jellyfish. As stated in a 1961 book, *Prehistoric Life on Earth*, "The invertebrate animal phyla are all represented in Cambrian deposits...."[4] It was then believed that vertebrates had not appeared until the Lower Ordovician, but in 1977 fully developed heterostracan vertebrate fish fossils were discovered in the Upper Cambrian of Wyoming. The discovery, reported in *Science* magazine, May 5, 1978, placed every major animal phylum (group) in the Cambrian rocks.[5] This extremely significant information comes as quite a shock to most people for it is not discussed in school or in university textbooks. The museum officials, however, freely talked about the explosive appearance of complex life in the Cambrian rocks.

They explained that the sudden appearance of all animal phyla with no ancestors was called the "Cambrian Explosion." Dr. Eldredge of the American Museum of Natural History said, "There is still a tremendous problem with the sudden diversification of multicellular life. There is no question about that. That's a real phenomenon." He said that it could not be explained away with the assertion that the ancestors of Cambrian life all had soft parts and thus left no fossils, and he was not going to give a scenario of why he thought that explosion took place. Jellyfish, for example, have very soft parts and yet they left distinct fossils in the Cambrian rocks. Nor can the Cambrian explosion be explained away with the assumption that Precambrian rocks were all destroyed somehow by metamorphism or erosion, for, as Dr. Eldredge said, "Certainly that has been refuted. I think the pattern is real. What we see there is not a function of the rotten record — it's a real biological problem. It's just that I'm kinda loath to make up stories about it. We have a real problem with testability." Up to 5,000 feet of Precambrian rocks grade continuously into the Cambrian in places with no sign of a nonconformity (long intervening period of erosion).

Noted evolutionist Dr. George Gaylord Simpson has called the sudden appearance of many types of complex life forms in the Cambrian rocks the "major mystery of the history of life."[6] He said that two-thirds of evolution was already over by the time we find the first fossils. Today some evolutionists are saying that 75% of the evolutionary process occurred before the first fossils were deposited.

T.N. George admitted the same when he stated, "Granted an evolutionary origin of the main groups of animals, and not an act of special creation, the absence of any record whatsoever of a single member of any of the phyla in the Precambrian rocks remains as inexplicable on orthodox grounds as it was to Darwin."[7]

Regarding the Precambrian-Cambrian boundary and whether any multicelled ancestors appear below it, Dr. Raup said, "Well, much depends upon how you define the boundary between the Precambrian and Cambrian. This has gone through several phases. There was a time when people were identifying as multicellular life a whole bunch of things which subsequently have been shown to be purely inorganic. For example, there is one classic case where ripple-marked sand which had been mud-cracked and the interference of these patterns produced some very strange wormlike things.... These things have been described as Precambrian metazoans (multicelled) several times but it was clearly shown a long time ago that they are not fossils. This kind of thing is a pseudofossil....For a long time these were the only Precambrian fossils known, but one after the other they have been debunked."

Dr. Raup said that in the mid-fifties microfossils of algae were found along the north shore of Lake Superior. These were called "stromatolites" and were the first microfossils about which there was a consensus of agreement. Then in the late fifties, William Schoph did a thesis on bacteria in the Bitter Springs formation of Australia. Since that time the pseudofossils have been debunked and forgotten. Also, in the fifties, Glaessner described impressions of metazoan fossils in the "extremely late Precambrian rocks" called Ediacaran of Australia. Dr. Raup said that you could call them 600 million years old compared to 570 million for the start of the Cambrian. There is a consensus that these are the first multicelled fossils.

How did Dr. Raup explain the sudden so-called explosion of very complex life forms in the Cambrian? Are all major phyla including chordates, subphylum vertebrates, found in the Cambrian? He said, "In the Upper Cambrian perhaps. There is no question that the major invertebrate faunas come in with a rush." He explained this by saying that he had a "hunch" that "evolution is capable of moving at a colossal rate." In other words, today evolution is moving at such a slow rate that it cannot be observed, but in the past it moved at such a rapid rate that it left no evidences in the fossil record.

It was pointed out to Dr. Raup that Simpson had said that two-thirds of evolution was over by the time we find the first fossils. Creationists were saying that, to an open-minded person, this would indicate agreement between the creation model and what was found in Cambrian rocks. You have to make up stories to fill in the gaps. He replied, "Sure. It's a process of rationalization. No question about it."

What did Dr. Raup think about the standard textbook explanations for the Cambrian explosion — that all the Precambrian rocks were metamorphosed or eroded away and therefore you do not find any ancestors of the complex life forms? He said that this was an old idea, called the Laplalian interval, that there was a hiatus in the record. "That won't wash. The record is complete enough in enough areas over that boundary that we can't use that anymore." Unfortunately, the people who write public school textbooks on earth science are not aware of this change in paradigm. The author of a widely used textbook for Regents Earth Science in New York State told the author in 1978 that he still used this outmoded explanation.

In 1982 Preston Cloud and Martin Glaessner wrote an article for *Science* magazine in which they described 26 species in 18 genera and 4 or more phyla of metazoans that had been found in the Ediacaran deposits.[8] Whether these rocks should be classified as Cambrian or very late Precambrian is open to argument, but their classification is irrelevant. The important question is whether the organisms they contain had any candidate ancestors and whether they could have been the ancestors to the hard-bodied Cambrian creatures.

The February 1984 issue of *Natural History* magazine contains a long article by Dr. Gould on the Ediacaran formation in Australia. He contends in it that every animal in that formation shares a basic mode of organization quite distinct from the architecture of living groups as well as from the Cambrian creatures. He said that the Cambrian creatures represent the complete replacement of Ediacaran forms after a mass extinction, not simply an improvement, so the Ediacaran animals could not have been the ancestors of the Cambrian creatures since the former were ribbon-shaped and pancake-shaped soft-bodied animals, completely different than the latter hard-bodied forms. Dr. Gould wrote, "I regard the failure to find a clear 'vector of progress' in life's history as the most puzzling fact of the fossil record."[9] It of course would be no puzzle at all if he had not decided before

he examined the evidence that common-ancestry evolution
was a fact, "like apples falling from the trees," and that we
can only permit ourselves to discuss possible mechanisms to
explain that assumed fact.

Dr. Patterson said that he knew of no fossils before the
Ediacaran formation. "Of course there is argument about
some of them, particularly the earliest ones, that these aren't
fossils at all, that they are inorganic things. Perhaps it is
correct that they are inorganic."

New Scientist magazine of 15 October 1981 reported that the
rocks previously believed to contain the oldest evidence of
life, the 3.8 billion-year-old Isua outcrop in Greenland, were
found to contain only weathered crystals. The article said:

> Further analysis of the world's oldest rocks has
> confirmed that microscopic inclusions are *not* the
> fossilised remains of living cells; instead they are
> crystals of dolomite-type carbonates, rusted by
> water that has seeped into the rock.[10]

New York's state paleontologist, Dr. Donald Fisher, talked
about the Precambrian rocks of New York. As to why there
was a lack of Precambrian fossils, he said, "The Precambrian
are metamorphosed so the chances of finding fossils would
be very remote."

He was asked about how he identified Cambrian rocks:
"Then you date these rocks strictly by the fossils they contain?
You don't have any radiometric dating for the paleo rocks?"
He replied:

> That's right for the Cambrian rocks. We do have
> radiometric dates for other rocks in the column but
> not in the Cambrian. All of our Cambrian rocks
> are sedimentary rocks. In adjacent Massachusetts
> and Vermont there are metamorphic Cambrian
> rocks, and there are also some very small igneous
> (lava) dikes of Cambrian age. Most of our diag-
> nostic fossils for correlation purposes are trilobites
> ....In fact most of the Cambrian is zoned on the
> basis of trilobites. There are other fossils in the
> Cambrian rocks but they are not useful as yet for
> correlation purposes. We don't know enough about

them. There are strange looking things in the Cambrian which don't have an affinity with the organisms living today. Many of the fossils in the Cambrian are phosphatic. This is a little puzzling because no other portion of the geologic time scale has as large a portion of phosphatic fossils as the Cambrian does. Whether the shelly fossils had not yet developed their calcium carbonate shells at the time, we don't know.

Dr. Fisher explained that a phosphatic fossil is one that contains calcium phosphate shells rather than calcium carbonate. He explained the sequence in which the trilobites are found: "For example, in eastern New York, in Columbia County, we have the Germantown formation which is in part Cambrian and the other part Ordovician. We have a number of sequences of trilobites here and other fossils. We are not always that fortunate and have to do piecemeal stratigraphy so-called. We take a section from one area and dovetail it with a section from another area."

Dr. Fisher said that he could not explain why there were no soft-bodied creatures found fossilized in New York Cambrian deposits although four of the fifteen soft-bodied animal phyla were reported in the July 1979 issue of *Scientific American* magazine in the Burgess Shale Cambrian of Canada.[11] He said, "We do have some a little higher up in the Ordovician that are thought to be jellyfish." Besides trilobites we have tubes of worms and, "We have no corals in the Cambrian and a few brachiopods. No crinoids. We have algae . . . we do have stromatolites that look like fossil cabbages. We have fossil snails—only the shells. We have no clams, bryozoans or cephalopods in the Cambrian here."

Question: "All of the Precambrian here is metamorphosed, but in some other places doesn't the Precambrian grade continuously for 5,000 feet or more into the Cambrian?"

Dr. Fisher answered, "Right. In the southern Appalachians in particular, and one of the best examples is in Glacier Park. They have thousands of feet of sedimentary rock beneath the bottom trilobite zone. There are other places in Siberia where it goes down thousands of meters below the lowest trilobite zone into unmetamorphosed rock. So the placement of the base of the Cambrian is a real problem."

Does Dr. Fisher agree with Dr. Cloud's statement in the November 1973 *Geology* magazine that no multicelled creatures have been found fossilized in the Precambrian? Answer:

> I don't know if I can agree or disagree. I don't care much where they put the base of the Cambrian. It is a very arbitrary placement. As long as a committee of experts decides once and for all where they are going to put it, fine. Right now there are many differences of opinion so if someone talks about the Cambrian we aren't sure if they are talking about the lowest trilobite zones or something else.

How deep below the surface does the Paleozoic extend in New York State? Dr. Fisher said, "The deepest well is the Olin well in western New York and that has gone down about 12,000 feet. They were pretty close to the bottom of the Paleozoic in the Potsdam sandstone. That was a dry hole."

Nature magazine reported in a 6 January 1983 article entitled ''Numerical Dating of Precambrian-Cambrian Boundary:''

> The Precambrian-Cambrian boundary is important because it is at the base of the Cambrian that the fossil record documents the first explosive event in the evolution of life....There is no agreement yet concerning either a lithostratigraphical (stratotype) nor a biostratigraphical (biozonal) definition of the boundary.[12]

Several conferences were held during 1983 in an attempt to resolve the problem of establishing a consensus on how to identify the base of the Cambrian. For instance, the May 7, 1983 *Science News* magazine reported on a forthcoming meeting that month of a committee of the International Geological Correlation Project for "the naming of a 'golden spike' for the Cambrian-Precambrian boundary....On the fourth day discussion will be suspended as the scientists vote, establishing a reference point for all future studies of the Cambrian-Precambrian boundary. 'I don't think we're going to have an easy time,' says Allison Palmer of the Geological Society of America. 'We're all going to go away unhappy in varying degrees.' '' The article proceeded to explain the problem:

> Below the boundary there are almost no skeletal fossils, only traces where soft-bodied, multicellular animals, or metazoans, burrowed or left imprints in sediments as old as 650 million years or older....
> With the appearance of preservable hard parts the Cambrian period and the familiar fossil record began....Within a few tens of millions of years... nearly all major forms of life known today had appeared in the fossil record. This rampant proliferation of life forms is called the "Cambrian explosion."[13]

The article said that some sequences, such as in the Grand Canyon of Arizona and other places, "show an abrupt 'discontinuity' or change in the record of life....Rock layers containing evidence of soft-bodied animals are missing, and it appears that shelly animals evolved with no obvious precursors."

The 16 September 1983 issue of *New Scientist* also frankly discussed the Cambrian explosion:

> One feature of the fossil record that puzzled 19th century geologists was the rocks below a certain level seemed to be devoid of fossils of animal or plant remains. The lowest obviously fossil-bearing deposits, which the geologists first identified in Wales, they assigned to the Cambrian period... living things were well established by the beginning of the Cambrian.[14]

Referring to the 3.8 billion-year-old rocks in Greenland, the article said, "Geologists have found no conclusive evidence of life in these Greenland rocks...."

Did the geology conferences of 1983 resolve the problem and succeed in driving the "golden spike" at the base of the Cambrian? Certainly not. There was just as much disagreement in January 1984 as there was a year before.

The conclusion one might draw from this confusing picture

of how specialists identify the base of the Cambrian is that
they use one or more of the following criteria:

1. The lowest fossil-bearing rocks in Cambria,
   Wales
2. The lowest trilobite zone
3. The lowest multicelled organisms
4. The lowest hard-shelled organisms
5. Where a committee votes to place it
6. 570 to 650 million years ago
7. The lowest obviously fossil-bearing deposits

Although all of these have been used as criteria for identifying the base of Cambrian rocks, there is no consensus on any
one of them. Criteria numbers three and seven cannot be used
because, at one place or another in the world, rocks of every
geologic period lay directly on basement rocks below which
there are no fossils.

So there is no evidence whatsoever of how a single-celled
organism might have converted into multicelled organisms.
The metazoa just abruptly appear in the fossil record with
every organ and structure complete. Some of the most complex structures are present in the Cambrian organisms, such as
the eye of the squid, which is very similar to the human eye.

The squid eye, with its lens, pupil, and optic nerve, is obviously fully functional, and there is no evidence that a light-
sensitive spot on the skin gradually generated these highly
complicated and coordinated features. Also, the various
trilobites found in the Cambrian already possessed very complex eyes. Evolutionists admit that trilobites would have had to
evolve eyes separately about 30 or 40 different times since they
had such distinctively different types of eyes.

Paley made much of the intricacy and perfection of the eye,
and said that it could have no other interpretation than that it
was not the product of chance. In fact, he began his book with
this very point. Since Darwin was quite familiar with Paley's
book, it is no wonder that he wrote that the eye turned him
cold all over when he pondered its origin. He said:

> To suppose that the eye with all its inimitable
> contrivances for adjusting the focus to different
> distances, for admitting different amounts of light,

and for the correction of spherical and chromatic aberration, could have been formed by natural selection, seems, I confess, absurd in the highest degree.[15]

Certainly, Darwin knew that the eye could not have been the product of an accident — especially not an explosion, Cambrian or otherwise.

So the picture has not really changed since the time of Charles Darwin except to become even more vivid in revealing a lack of evidence for ancestors to Cambrian life. The enigma is the same as Darwin candidly admitted in *The Origin:*

> To the question why we do not find rich fossiliferous deposits belonging to these assumed earliest periods prior to the Cambrian system, I can give no satisfactory answer.[16]

Origin of First Living Cell

What is the evidence that a single living cell came into existence spontaneously from nonliving chemicals? Most books and articles on evolution begin by conjecturing about the origin of the first ancestral living cell. They usually refer to experiments that any advanced chemistry student can perform in the laboratory to form the ingredients of life, that is, amino acids, from four gases. The now famous Miller-Orgel experiment in which methane, ammonia, water vapor, and hydrogen were circulated in a closed apparatus in the presence of an electrical spark simply produced a few weak amino acids when a trap was used to protect the products. Then Sidney Fox of the University of Miami heated pure amino acids at 175 degrees Centigrade for six to ten hours and formed globules that resembled drops of oil floating on water. He boasted that he had practically formed life in a test tube. Have these and similar experiments produced anything remotely resembling a living cell or even a significant amount of the necessary ingredients of a reproducing living cell?

In the first place, although the Miller experiment has been given great acclaim in textbooks and the establishment scientific community for over thirty years, recent discoveries about the atmospheres of other planets coupled with the discovery of carbon dioxide and oxidized iron bands in Precambrian rocks have seriously challenged its basic assumptions. The Miller experiment simulated a reducing atmosphere with no free oxygen because the presence of free oxygen would have been highly destructive to the products of the experiment, thus preventing their formation. These recent discoveries have indicated that there was some free oxygen present in the early atmosphere, so evolutionists must come up with a new scenario for the spontaneous formation of life on Earth.

Nobel Prize-winner and codiscoverer of DNA, Francis Crick, recognized the problem of getting life to form spontaneously on Earth if oxygen were present. When he wrote the book *Life Itself* in 1981, evidence for oxygen in the earliest Precambrian rocks was just beginning to be discussed. He wrote:

> If it turns out that the early atmosphere was not reducing but contained a fair amount of oxygen, then the picture is more complicated. . . . If this were really true, it would support the idea of Directed Panspermia, because planets elsewhere in the universe may have had a more reducing atmosphere and thus have on them a more favorable prebiotic soup.[17]

Professor Carl Sagan agrees with this, for in a lengthy discussion following the author's lecture at Cornell University on April 24, 1984, he said:

> If there were free oxygen in the early atmosphere of the Earth before the development of green plants, we would have a serious contradiction.

Dr. Sagan said that he was not aware of the evidences for oxygen there, however.

In commenting on the great improbability of the spontaneous generation of a reproducing system, Dr. Crick wrote:

> What is so frustrating for our present purpose is that it seems almost impossible to give any numerical value to the probability of what seems a rather unlikely sequence of events. . . . An honest man, armed with all the knowledge available to us now,

> could only state that in some sense, the origin of life
> appears at the moment to be almost a miracle....
> But if it turns out that it was rather unlikely, then
> we are compelled to consider whether it might have
> arisen in other places in the Universe where possibly,
> for one reason or another, conditions were more
> favorable.[18]

Dr. Crick's concept of Directed Panspermia is that the first living cell must have been transported by rocket ship on a 10,000-year voyage from some other planet outside our solar system.[19] Because of his prestige, his acceptance of the Panspermia theory has caused great consternation in the establishment scientific community. This shatters the very foundation of arguments for the evolution of life on Earth. If first life could not have evolved spontaneously on Earth, then that definitely removes the question from the realm of science. We cannot even observe a single planet outside our solar system, much less examine evidence that life evolved there.

Some geochemists contend that the presence of carbon dioxide does not necessarily mean that the early atmosphere contained free oxygen, but there are many who feel that all of the evidences considered together provide strong justification for the conclusion. As reported in *New Scientist*, 13 May 1982, "Astronomers and geophysicists now seem to be reaching agreement on their interpretation of the early atmosphere." This article also said that the gases released by volcanoes today are dominated by water vapor and carbon dioxide, and there is no reason to believe that the volatile products of earlier volcanic activity would have been substantially different. Since both Venus and Mars have atmospheres of carbon dioxide, why would the early Earth likewise not have had an atmosphere containing carbon dioxide? The article said that this ridiculed the old idea of a reducing atmosphere:

> It used to be widely thought, and widely taught,
> that the original 'primitive' atmosphere of the early
> Earth was a 'reducing' atmosphere.... The reason-
> ing behind this assumption developed primarily
> from the belief that such an atmosphere would be
> ideal, and might be essential, for the development

of the complex nonliving molecules that preceded
life.... This picture captured the popular imagination, and the story of life emerging in the seas or
pools of a planet swathed in an atmosphere of
methane and ammonia soon became part of the
scientific folklore that 'every schoolchild knows.'

Indeed, this is still taught in 1984 in most schools and universities. The article continued:

But now, this particular card house seems to have
been demolished, and a new scientific edifice is
arising in its place. In order to convince people that
the Earth started out with a reduced, not a reducing,
atmosphere — that is, one with oxygen already
locked up in gases such as carbon dioxide, and
which cannot take up more oxygen — astronomers,
geophysicists and, more recently, climatologists
have had to explain how life could arise on a wet
planet with a carbon-dioxide atmosphere laced with
traces of ammonia. By such devious routes is scientific process made.[20]

As early as July 1980, *New Scientist* magazine printed an
article on the subject:

Although biologists concerned with the origin of
life often quote an early atmosphere consisting of
reduced gases, this seems as much from ignorance of
recent advances as from active opposition to
them.... The time has come, it seems, to accept as
the new orthodoxy the idea of early oxidized atmospheres on all three terrestrial planets, and the
biological primers which still tell of life on Earth
starting out from a methane/ammonia atmosphere
energized by electric storms and solar ultraviolet
need to be rewritten.[21]

Gradually the scientific literature is grudgingly presenting
articles that acknowledge the complete reversal on the con-
sistency of the early atmosphere. The March 1982 issue of
Geology magazine contained the following:

Geologic evidence often presented in favor of an
early anoxic atmosphere is both contentious and

ambiguous....Recent biological and interplanetary studies seem to favor an early oxidized atmosphere rich in carbon dioxide and possibly containing free molecular oxygen....It is suggested that
from the time of the earliest dated rocks at 3.7 b.y.
ago, Earth had an oxygenic atmosphere.[22]

The April 1984 issue of *Scientific American* reported on an
international conference of the Precambrian Paleobiology
Research Group that reviewed the latest thinking on the
Precambrian atmosphere. Although it concluded that there
was not a lot of oxygen present, the report said, "It was not,
however, oxygen free; the bands [oxidized iron] represent a
large sink for the reactive oxygen." It said that oxidized iron
bands appear at about the same time as the first bacterial
cells. Also, at about the same time that the first life appeared,
carbon dioxide was present, perhaps even abundant.[23]
Actually, the report said that the earliest rusted iron bands
were 3.8 billion years old and the oldest fossils of cells were 3.5
billion years old. So, according to this group of Precambrian
specialists, there is evidence of free oxygen at least 300 million
years before there were living cells.

According to John Gribbin, "All we have to do now is
rewrite all those textbooks and ensure that 'every schoolchild
knows' what the best theory of the evolution of the Earth's
atmosphere and the origins of life is today...."[24]

Sir Fred Hoyle, famous British mathematician and astron-
omer who originated the steady-state theory of nucleogenesis
(formation of the universe), published a book in 1981, *Evolution from Space*, in which he reversed himself on the origin
of life. He and co-author Chandra Wickramasinghe stated
that, although atheists all their lives, they had come to the
conclusion that the high degree of order and specificity in the
universe demanded pre-existing intelligence, even to the limit
of God. They wrote:

Once we see, however, that the probability of life
originating at random is so utterly miniscule as to
make it absurd, it becomes sensible to think that the
favourable properties of physics, on which life
depends, are in every respect deliberate....It is,

therefore, almost inevitable that our own measure
of intelligence must reflect higher intelligences...
even to the limit of God.[25]

They had come to this conclusion because of their determination of the statistical improbabilities of a single cell originating in the primitive atmosphere in the assumed 4.6 billion
years of Earth's history. According to their calculations, the
probability of life originating by random processes was one
chance in 10^{40000}. Explaining how evolutionists get around this
insurmountable problem, they said:

> The tactic is to argue that although the chance of
> arriving at the biochemical system of life as we know
> it is admitted to be utterly miniscule, there is in
> Nature such an enormous number of other chemical
> systems which could also support life that any old
> planet like the Earth would inevitably arrive
> sooner or later at one or another of them.
>
> This argument is the veriest nonsense, and if it
> is to be imbibed at all it must be swallowed with a
> jorum of strong ale.[26]

Hoyle and Wickramasinghe call it "hand-waving" when
evolutionists attempt to side-step the difficulties by arguing
that the first enzymes in the first life were much shorter in
their peptide lengths than they are today.

Darwin recognized that the arguments for the origin of life
by chemical shuffling were weak when he wrote: "...if (and oh
what a big if) we could conceive in some warm little pond, with
all sorts of ammonia and phosphoric salts present, that a
protein compound was chemically formed ready to undergo
still more complex changes...."

Hoyle writes about this "big if": "As the enormity of the
supposition was slowly revealed in the present century, there
was an attempt to evade this difficulty through the invention
of pseudo-science."[27] The following excerpt from *Nature*
magazine, 12 November 1981, reported more startling statements by Hoyle on this subject:

> "The chance that higher life forms might have
> emerged in this way is comparable with the chance
> that a tornado sweeping through a junk-yard might

assemble a Boeing 747 from the materials therein." Of adherents of biological evolution, Hoyle said that he was at a loss to understand biologists' widespread compulsion to deny what seems to me to be obvious.[28]

What is so complicated about a single cell that would bring people who are philosophically committed to a mechanistic origin of life to take this position? Advancements in biology, such as the discovery of the genetic code by Watson and Crick, have shown beyond any doubt that the enormous information content of a single living cell is almost incomprehensible. As the *Encyclopedia Britannica* says, "The information content of a simple cell has been estimated as around 10^{12} bits...." This is the amount of data estimated to be contained in the DNA molecule of *E. coli,* the bacteria in our intestines that help digest our food. According to Carl Sagan, there are about a trillion letters in all of the books in the world's largest library.[29] Not only is this an impossible amount of data to have originated by random shuffling process, but the primordial Earth's atmosphere simply was not conducive to any imagined scenario for the spontaneous formation of the first living, reproducing cell.

It is interesting to note how prominent population geneticist and outspoken evolutionist Professor John Maynard Smith treated the origin of first life in his 1982 book, *Evolution Now*, which was supposed to be a report on the latest research relating to validating evolution theory.[30] Instead of producing an explanation of how life might have started from nonliving chemicals, he began his speculations with an enzyme that has only been observed to come from a living cell. Of course, he thought that an enzyme might somehow form spontaneously from other chemicals, but he did not produce any mathematical calculations showing the probability of this occurring in 4.6 billion years. Fred Hoyle's calculations showed that this simply could not be expected to happen in even 20 billion years and, with oxygen present in the early atmosphere, it would have been an even greater impossibility.

Anyway, Stephen Jay Gould says that there would have been far less time than 4.6 billion years for this highly improb-

able event to have occurred: "We are left with very little time
between the development of suitable conditions for life on the
Earth's surface and the origin of life. . . . Life apparently arose
about as soon as the Earth became cool enough to support
it."[31] The latest speculation is that life was present less than
one billion years after the formation of the Earth.

Fred Hoyle wrote in the 19 November 1981 *New Scientist*
that there are 2,000 complex enzymes required for a living
organism but not a single one of these could have formed on
Earth by random, shuffling processes in even 20 billion years:

> I don't know how long it is going to be before
> astronomers generally recognize that the combina-
> torial arrangement of not even one among the many
> thousands of biopolymers on which life depends
> could have been arrived at by natural processes here
> on the earth. Astronomers will have a little diffi-
> culty in understanding this because they will be
> assured by biologists that it is not so, the biologists
> having been assured in their turn by others that it
> is not so. The 'others' are a group of persons who
> believe, quite openly, in mathematical miracles.
> They advocate the belief that tucked away in nature,
> outside of normal physics, there is a law which per-
> forms miracles (provided the miracles are in the aid
> of biology). This curious situation sits oddly on a
> profession that for long has been dedicated to com-
> ing up with logical explanations of biblical miracles
> . . . . It is quite otherwise, however, with the modern
> miracle workers, who are always to be found living
> in the twilight fringes of thermodynamics.[32]

It is one thing to talk in generalities about such matters, but
still another to face the hard facts of the laws of probability.
The reason that the origin of the first reproducing cell is such
an important consideration when one evaluates theories of
origins is that the supposed creative force called "natural
selection" could not have played any part until there was
reproduction. When all of the extraneous verbiage is removed,
natural selection is nothing more than differential
reproduction, that is, more offspring are produced than are

required and only the better suited survive to reproduce. There is no conceivable way that this so-called "creative process" could have operated until there was such a thing as reproduction. And meaningful reproduction is known to exist only in a living organism containing complex enzymes, DNA, and RNA. Evolutionists have searched diligently for a self-replicating molecule that has been generated purely from inanimate matter, but their efforts have been in vain. Experiments that use segments of RNA and enzymes as raw material are impertinent for they obviously could not demonstrate how a reproducing cell might have formed spontaneously without first having the products of living organisms.

It is often stated by evolutionists that with enough time, anything could happen regardless of how improbable it might be. Nobel prize winner George Wald has said, "Time is the hero of the plot. Given enough time anything can happen — the impossible becomes probable, the improbable becomes certain."[33] Prominent evolutionist Julian Huxley has stated that, given enough time, monkeys typing on typewriters could eventually type out the complete works of Shakespeare. Such uninformed statements have a dramatic effect on the layman, and even persons who have the mathematical background to know better often fail to make the simple calculations that would reveal the ridiculousness of the conjecture. For example, if there were monkeys typing on typewriters covering every square foot of the Earth's surface and each one typed at random at the fantastic rate of ten characters a second for 30 billion years, there would not be the slightest reasonable chance that a single one would type out a single specific five word sentence of 31 letters, spaces, and punctuation. (The actual probability is less than one chance in a trillion.) Yet Huxley was permitted to make the preposterous statement that monkeys could type out the complete works of Shakespeare, and no evolutionary scientist or mathematician who knew better raised a single objection.

Time definitely is not the hero of the plot. In reality, time destroys the assumptions of evolution theory — even the 20 billion years assumed since the big bang. If a single five-word sentence could not be formed in more time than the Earth has existed, it is even less conceivable that the data contained in the genes of a single cell could have formed by random processes, because the genes of the simplest single-celled organism contain more data than there are letters in all of the volumes of the world's largest library.

Dr. Eldredge denied having any opinion about how the DNA code for the first living cell could have happened by accident. He said, "I have no opinion about that."

Regardless of these seemingly insurmountable problems, evolutionists assume that a single cell spontaneously formed from nonliving chemicals, and then it began to reproduce and make mistakes. They claim that with natural selection weeding out the bad reproductive mistakes and preserving the good, the process could have created the incredible amount of intelligence found in the biosphere.

Invertebrate to Vertebrate

What evidence is there in the fossil record of the origin of the subphylum vertebrata — animals with a spinal cord and backbone? Since vertebrate fishes just abruptly appear in the Cambrian deposits of Wyoming with no ancestors leading up to them, evolutionists freely admit that there is no evidence of their evolutionary origin from invertebrates. When asked about the origin of vertebrate fishes, Dr. Patterson, after a very long pause, stated, "Ten years ago I'd have been perfectly willing to tell you, but it so happens that I know someone who's been working on this problem for about 15 years — the starfish end of it — the echinoderms. He believes that this development can be traced from the Cambrian with the echinoderms. I could very easily refer you to his work and say that I agree with him that fish are related to echinoderms, but I do not think it is obvious." Most evolutionists admit that the gap between invertebrates with a hard ectoskeleton (outer shell) and vertebrates with a skeleton is the most obvious gap of all.

Did Dr. Raup accept the discovery in 1977 of heterostracan vertebrate fish in the Upper Cambrian of Wyoming as validated? He said that he was familiar with it and the people he talked with about it thought that it was "OK." As a matter of fact, that material had been in the Field Museum for awhile. Could he explain the origin of vertebrates, and what was his candidate transitional form between invertebrates and vertebrates? He said that he could not really say but that echinoderms, the group of which starfish are members, had been a likely candidate. But he said that this led back to the placing of question marks at the branch points. He said, "There is no direct documentation." No museum official offered any real fossil evidence that any one of the various invertebrates evolved into vertebrate fish.

Fish to Amphibian

Most scenarios on macroevolution say that the lobe-finned fish converted its fins into legs and feet, turning into an amphibian. As Carl Sagan said in his Cosmos television series, during a drought in the Devonian period a fish found it very convenient to have evolved feet and legs so it could walk overland when its swamp dried up.[34] The crossopterygian lobe-finned fish was supposed to have evolved into the ichthyostegid amphibian about 250 million years ago. Is there any evidence of this transformation in the fossil record?

When asked by the author if he was comfortable about the story that the lobe-finned fish turned into an amphibian, Dr. Patterson evaded a direct reply with, "I'm working on it." To the question about whether he thought the crossopterygian was the ancestor of the ichthyostegid amphibian, Dr. Patterson answered, "I have questions about that....It is futile to be looking for answers to questions which we have no way of answering."

Dr. Eldredge, when asked about the fish-to-amphibian transition said, "That I know nothing about." Dr. Raup said that he only knew what he read about that transition. At the time he was a paleontologist and chairman of the Geology Department at the Field Museum as well as curator of geology there so if there were any evidence of evolutionary transitions in the fossil record he should have had firsthand knowledge of them. Initially, he said that he thought "there are fish today that can walk." But Dr. Raup just chuckled when it was pointed out that an evolutionist had claimed during a debate that fossilized fish footprints had been found, and he had been forced to admit his error since fish had never been found with feet and legs.

When Dr. Raup was asked if he knew of any transitional forms at all, he just sat in silence. After a long pause the questioning was continued, "Transitions in the fossil record, that is? I don't mean slight variations in birds' beaks or coloration in moths. I think I could make a good case for connecting up some living species like dogs, wolves, jackals and coyotes since they are all interfertile and produce fertile offspring. But, in the fossil record, do you see any transitions?" To this Dr. Raup sat for ten seconds and gave no answer. Later, after other questions he said, "There is a problem here that bothers me. I certainly agree with Patterson that the large question of the origin of a dozen to twenty big groups — that it's very tough to determine the relationship of those."

When asked if he knew of any fish growing feet and legs, any transitional forms, Dr. Fisher replied, "Any transitional forms? I'm not a paleoichthyologist so I wouldn't want to comment on that." He was told that no one else who had been interviewed would comment either so he should not feel bad. Dr. Patterson was the only one who was a paleoichthyologist and qualified to analyze fish fossils, but the other museum officials were certainly capable of reporting what their museums had on display and what other specialists had to offer as examples of intermediate forms. None of the museum officials could produce any fossil evidence of an intermediate ancestor connecting the amphibians with fishes.

Dr. Fisher was asked if he thought the fossil fish found in Upper Cambrian rocks of Wyoming, as reported in the May 5, 1978 *Science* magazine, were actually heterostracan vertebrate fish. He replied, "Yes. I happen to know the fellow who discovered it. He is John Repetski of the U.S. Geological Survey." Were they really vertebrates? He said, "I don't believe Mr. Repetski would have reported them as fish if they weren't .... When you analyze the reports of some of these things you have to know the person who is making the report. If I is a competent, reliable person that isn't looking for publicit that means a great deal."

Amphibian to Reptile

Is the picture any different regarding the first appearance of reptiles in the fossil record? When Dr. Eldredge was asked about the supposed amphibian-to-reptile transition he replied that some taxonomists say that there is no such thing as a reptile. Dr. Eldredge continued, "And in respect to amphibians, some biologists say there is no such thing as an amphibian, either." Thus, a frog is not an amphibian but either a fish or reptile. He said, "Well, the reptiles are not a natural group because some are more closely related to birds and some are more closely related to mammals." That is all he had to offer. So he side-stepped the question by suggesting in the third person that there was no such thing as a reptile. In other words, according to this contention, the reptiles such as alligators, snakes, turtles, *Tyrannosaurus rex*, and *Brontosaurus* should all be called birds or mammals. It is highly unlikely that a prominent scientist such as Dr. Eldredge would make such meaningless statements if there were any actual fossils connecting amphibians with reptiles.

Neither Dr. Patterson nor Dr. Raup could offer a single transitional form between any of the major groups of animals. They did not comment specifically about the origin of reptiles. Dr. Fisher answered the question of the appearance of reptiles: "Reptiles are in the Carboniferous."

Question: About the same time as amphibians?

Fisher: The amphibians are a bit older. Amphibians from Greenland are in the Devonian.

Question: Reptiles are there. Now, what we are looking for is any indication of ancestry. We do find nests of fossilized hard-shelled dinosaur eggs. Right?

Fisher: Now there are some forms that the vertebrate paleontologists have a hard time in classifying as amphibians or reptiles. Some of those are in Romer's book (*Vertebrate Paleontology*).[35]

Question: Yes, it has been pointed out that there is a difficulty in classifying certain skeletons. However, when you look at the egg of a frog or salamander and compare it with the hard-shelled amniote egg of a reptile, you can see a revolution in structure. There is no question about the classification there.

Fisher: Yes.

Reply: When you look at the egg, to postulate a transition there stretches the imagination pretty far. The hard-shelled amniote egg is totally different from the soft egg of amphibians. The story in the textbooks that we teach the school students (I have to keep referring to this because a lot of misinformation has been given out and we are trying to correct that) is that during the Devonian, a drought came along and some inland fish had to walk overland to get to water. Over a period of 50 million years or so they grew feet and legs and then later a hard shell for their eggs. Now that sounds kind of far-fetched when you spell it out, but is that what the textbooks say really happened?

Fisher: Yes.

Reply: We don't want to put that in (science textbooks) if it's just imagination.

Fisher: Yes. As you say, the textbooks fail to distinguish whether you are talking about this change taking place in an individual or is it taking place over thousands of years in several generations.

Reply: No. I wouldn't fault them that way. No, I think the word that has gone out is that individuals don't evolve, populations evolve. That is clear. But let's face it, for a population to evolve, it too must contain some in-between forms. They can't just jump, at least not according to Simpson. Now, as you know, Drs. Gould and Eldredge (and before them in 1940, Dr. Goldschmidt) say that there are no in-between forms since we don't find them. It's not because of the record, it's not because of preservation problems, it's because there weren't any.

Fisher: Do they really say this?

Reply: Dr. Gould wrote in the June-July 1977, *Natural History* magazine, "The fossil record with its abrupt transitions offers no support for gradual change,..."[36] Of course, the idea that a reptile laid an egg and a bird was hatched from the egg was not science, as you well know.

Dr. Fisher answered, "Yes."

As will be shown later, Dr. Gould has made many public statements that are even more explicit about the lack of transitional forms in the fossil record.

Chapter 4

The Fossil Record —
Reptile to Man

Reptile to Bird

Many evolutionists believe that the most impressive evidence of an evolutionary transition is that indicating the conversion of a reptile into a bird. When the author participated in the production of six television programs at the British Royal Academy in London in June 1982 to commemorate the centennial of Charles Darwin's death, the fossil bird *Archaeopteryx* was offered by the evolutionist experts as one of the best evidences of common-ancestry evolution. (Two others were the peppered moths of England and Darwin's finches). Let us examine the fossil evidence for this assumed transition in considerable detail to try to determine if it is as compelling as evolutionists contend.

The author questioned Dr. Eldredge about the supposed conversion of scales into feathers since all birds (class Aves) have feathers and all reptiles have scales. He said that feathers were a neat evolutionary novelty and that the only things you have to work on are inventions. It is like tracing the history of manuscripts. Somebody makes a mistake in copying manuscripts and then the mistake is perpetuated. He said that this gives you insight into the historical lineage of that manuscript and the same thing is true with evolutionary inventions. He continued, "If you invent feathers, the supposition would be (which could be falsified) you'd see feathers and see the distribution of feathers and you'd guess that all of the things that have feathers are related." He admitted that this supposition could be wrong. Of course his comparing the supposed invention of feathers to typographical errors in manuscripts has no bearing on whether there was any actual evidence that feathers evolved from scales.

According to Dr. Eldredge the fossil bird *Archaeopteryx* shown in Figure 3 had some of the "advanced" characteristics of birds and retained a tremendous amount of "primitive" characteristics, like teeth.

He was asked, "Isn't that true of every subclass of vertebrates, some have teeth and some do not, so how could that show reptilian ancestry? Some fish have teeth and some don't; some amphibians have teeth and some don't. Other ancient birds had teeth, and some mammals have teeth and some don't. How could you classify teeth as reptilian?" He replied that he did not say they were reptilian, but that the teeth were primitive.

Then he was asked, "How about man; does the presence of teeth show him as primitive?" And he replied, "Sure." It was pointed out that children have been taught in school that *Archaeopteryx* was transitional because it had teeth and we do not want to put that sort of speculation in the textbooks if it proves nothing. He replied, "No you don't. You want to say that it is a primitive holdover."

The next question was, "Are man's teeth a primitive holdover? Are fishes' teeth a primitive holdover? They really don't say *anything* about reptilian ancestry." Dr. Eldredge replied, "I know. They are general. They don't tell you anything about the specific relationship with mammals or *any* group." In the interview he explained that man's teeth are primitive because we tend to lose them in old age, but he later deleted that statement when he edited the typed interview transcript.

Dr. Patterson said that *Archaeopteryx* "has simply become a patsy for wishful thinking." In a letter to this author dated 10 April 1979, Dr. Patterson said, "Is *Archaeopteryx* the ancestor of all birds? Perhaps yes, perhaps no. There is no way of answering the question."[1] On the 1982 British television series mentioned earlier, Dr. Patterson emphasized the same point — that *Archeopteryx* was not a good example of a transitional form.

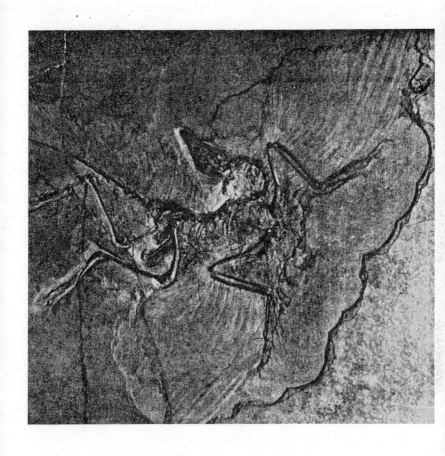

Figure 3. Archaeopteryx, the showcase of a transitional form, is now admitted by leading evolutionists not to be on the direct line between reptiles and birds because it is preceded by modern bird fossils.

This kind of information would be most helpful if it were made available to public school, college, and university, students when they attempt to unravel the great puzzle of which theory of origins they should use as the basis for their philosophy of life.

Dr. Fisher was asked, "Do you know anything about that, how feathers might have arisen from scales?" He replied, "None whatsoever."

Dr. Raup felt that the problem with *Archaeopteryx* was that our classification system forced us to put it in one box or the other. He said that if there were no intermediate category in our taxonomic system, our taxonomic tradition forced us to put something like *Archaeopteryx* in one class or the other. It was then pointed out to him, "But if it had half a feather, we'd be very glad to throw out the classification system. Nobody I've ever heard debating has ever used the ground rule that the only way we'll accept a transition is within the present classification system. Dr. Gish says it would take only five or six of these truly in-between forms with partial structures to document evolution. Anybody on either side investigating this thing, if they found a transitional form that had a partially formed or evolved organ or structure, would be very happy to say, 'You've got one for your side.' I would. I'm looking for that." Dr. Raup replied that, according to John Ostrom's current thinking about *Archaeopteryx*, in a sense the wings of *Archaeopteryx* were half-formed wings.

A report in *Science* magazine, 9 March 1979 was then handed to Dr. Raup with the comment: "This shows that the primary feathers (flight feathers on wings) of *Archaeopteryx* were asymmetrical and identical to those of modern flying birds. In nonflying birds such as the emu and ostrich, the primary feathers are symmetrical. Thus, specialists say that *Archaeopteryx* flew. That supersedes some of the earlier statements that it was just a dinosaur with feathers."[2] Dr. Raup replied, "OK, I heard Ostrom talk about this at a lecture series in Chicago. It is his contention that they were used for trapping, not for flying but trapping."

This is correct because Dr. John Ostrom of Yale University, a recognized world authority on the origin of birds, described his trapping theory in an article in the January/February 1979 issue of *American Scientist* magazine. He showed a sketch of a dinosaur that was growing wing feathers and using them for catching insects. See Figure 4. He felt that this was a much more plausible sounding scenario than the one about dinosaurs initially growing feathers as an insulation blanket.[3] In 1982 the British Museum of Natural History in London included this insect-catching explanation in their display on the origin of birds.

One reason the insect-trapping preadaption scenario was invented was because of the publicity being given to the reptile-to-bird transition by those criticizing the gradualistic idea of evolution. As mentioned earlier, Schindewolf and Goldschmidt had first brought attention to the problems of gradualism when they tried to escape from the quandary by proposing that a reptile laid an egg and a bird was hatched from the egg — twice in the same area and the same generation so there could be reproduction. Creationists drew much attention to the great difficulty evolutionists were having when they tried to invent plausible stories of how a reptile could have gradually developed the host of coordinated structures of birds.

This insect-catching scenario postulates that a population of dinosaurs gradually frayed out their foreleg and tail scales, somehow getting flight feathers with a rigid center shaft and hundreds of delicate parallel barbs running out from it. These contained thousands of little barbules to hook them together making an effective air seal. As the dinosaur dashed about in the underbrush chasing insects, it was able to keep these delicate new inventions from getting broken so that there was a selective advantage for the feathers to gradually become larger and larger. The dinosaurs with smaller foreleg feathers, according to the story, died off due to the competition for insects leaving only those with large feathers to survive. At the same time, the dinosaurs necessarily developed a host of other highly coordinated structures, that prepared it for flight. Then one day it must have found that it was all ready for its maiden flight: It had a foreleg that was shaped like an airfoil nicely streamlined with curvature in the proper direction to

Figure 4. Evolutionists speculate that reptiles did not develop feathers initially for flying, instead, they might have invented them for some entirely different purpose such as for catching insects.

generate lift; its bones were hollow; its center of gravity was located precisely for perfect stability in the air (about 25% of the way back from the front edge of the foreleg); its scales had thousands of barbs and barbules all evenly hooked together to keep the air from leaking through; it had perching feet; the scales on its tail were also converted into feathers for steering and balance; it had somehow developed the intricate skill to coordinate the action of all of these structures in flight; then it took off and became a flying bird. So the story goes.

But, in the game of evolutionary speculation, nothing seems to endure very long except the sacrosanct common-ancestry assumption. The scenario of preadaption by trapping insects generated so much tongue-in-cheek comment and outright embarrassment that others wrestling with the origin of birds problem decided to change the story again. On 1 July 1983 *Science* magazine published an article by Roger Lewin about some work by a group at Flagstaff, Arizona, that was supposed to have solved the whole problem. He made the surprising statement: "Unlike other major hypotheses on the origin of flight...there is no requirement for a leap of faith at any point."[4]

The Flagstaff group had written a very simple mathematical model of a flying object. This looked most impressive to natural scientists and others not familiar with aerodynamics and the complexity of getting a nonflying animal into the air by its development of flapping flight through purely random processes. The main discussion was restricted to an argument about whether reptiles learned to fly by dashing along the ground and gliding or climbing up into a tree and jumping off like a parachutist. This work is not expected to make an enduring contribution to the field of testable science, and a person knowledgeable about the complexities of flight must puzzle over the statement. It is difficult to understand how scenarios that cannot be tested can be transformed into certainty without a "leap of faith" somewhere along the line.

Even John Ostrom abandoned the insect-trapping story in 1983. An article by Roger Lewin in the 1 July 1983 issue of *Science* magazine quoted him as saying that he had given up on that idea. The last two lines of the article were: " 'Yes,' says

Ostrom, 'The insect net idea is dead. It did its job.' "[5] Apparently Ostrom felt that the job at hand was to confuse the opposition and convince the public and millions of students that birds had actually evolved from reptiles regardless of the fact that there was no scientific evidence of such a transition or any plausible mechanism for it.

Now Dr. Ostrom is agreeing with the idea that the origin of birds can be explained by the proposition that they started as a ground-running biped reptile that gradually grew feathers and all the other complex integrated features as it dashed and leaped along the ground. This is in contrast with the idea that birds began as tree-living animals that became aviators through first making short gliding flights or even parachuting to the ground.

Evolutionist author Francis Hitching included a detailed discussion of *Archaeopteryx* in his 1982 book, *The Neck of the Giraffe — Where Darwin Went Wrong*.[6] Referring to the oft-repeated claim that this fossil bird "proved beyond any argument" that there existed an animal with both reptilian and bird features, he wrote that the case is not so unambiguous as the claims make out: "Every one of its supposed reptilian features can be found in various species of undoubted birds." He discussed these six features of *Archaeopteryx:*

1. **It had a long bony tail, like a reptile's.**

In the embryonic stage, some living birds have more tail vertebrae than *Archaeopteryx*. They later fuse to become an upstanding bone called the pygostyle. The tail bone and feather arrangement on swans are very similar to those of *Archaeopteryx*. One authority claims that there is no basic difference between the ancient and modern forms: the difference lies only in the fact that the caudal vertebrae are greatly prolonged. But this does not make a reptile.

2. **It had claws on its feet and on its feathered forelimbs.**

However, many living birds such as the hoatzin in South America, the touraco in Africa and the ostrich also have claws. In 1983, the British Museum of Natural History displayed numerous species within nine families of birds with claws on the wings.

3. It had teeth.

Modern birds do not have teeth but many ancient birds did, particularly those in the Mesozoic. There is no suggestion that these birds were transitional. The teeth do not show the connection of *Archaeopteryx* with any other animal since every subclass of vertebrates has some with teeth and some without.

4. It had a shallow breastbone.

Various modern flying birds such as the hoatzin have similarly shallow breastbones, and this does not disqualify them from being classified as birds. And there are, of course, many species of nonflying birds, both living and extinct.

Recent examination of *Archaeopteryx's* feathers has shown that they are the same as those of modern birds that are excellent fliers. Dr. Ostrom says that there is no question that they are the same as the feathers of modern birds. They are asymmetrical with a center shaft and parallel barbs like those of today's flying birds.

5. Its bones were solid, not hollow, like a bird's.

This idea has been refuted because the long bones of *Archaeopteryx* are now known to be hollow.

6. It predates the general arrival of birds by millions of years.

This also has been refuted by recent paleontological discoveries. In 1977 a geologist from Brigham Young University, James A. Jensen, discovered in the Dry Mesa quarry of the Morrison formation in western Colorado a fossil of an unequivocal bird in Lower Jurassic rock. This deposit is dated as 60-million-years older than the Upper Jurassic rock in which *Archaeopteryx* was found. He first found the rear-leg femur and, later, the remainder of the skeleton. This was reported in *Science News* 24 September 1977. Professor John Ostrom commented, "It is obvious we must now look for the ancestors of flying birds in a period of time much older than that in which *Archaeopteryx* lived."[7]

At a conference in 1983, Professor Ostrom stated, "It is

highly improbable that *Archaeopteryx* is actually on the main line (to modern birds)."[8] It will be interesting to see if textbook writers begin to retract their previous dogmatic statements about *Archaeopteryx* being the best available showcase example of an intermediate form that documents the transition of one species into a basically different species with grossly different structures and functions.

In a debate in Tampa, Florida, Dr. Kenneth Miller stated that modern birds have little bumps, called nodes, on the wing bones where feathers are attached, but *Archaeopteryx* didn't have these so it was supposedly more reptilian than modern birds.[9] This is a fallacious argument. It is true that some birds, like the robin and barn owl, have an easily detectable row of bumps along the aft side of the ulna wing bones. But it is also true that the bumps are much less prominent in other living birds like the screech owl and, in some, like the chicken, they are not visible at all. This argument is obviously impertinent since domesticated birds like the chicken are assumed to have been derived from wild birds which are supposed to have evolved from the reptiles. Even schoolboys have learned that it is not difficult to become trapped in inconsistencies when you start making up stories.

Reptile to Mammal

Most books and museum displays on evolution state that mammals originated from reptiles with the insect eaters, called insectivores, being the first true mammals. Both the placental and marsupial mammals, they contend, evolved in parallel from the reptiles since they have such distinctively different reproductive systems.

There is a significant difference between reptiles and mammals. Reptiles lay eggs which have hard shells and they have scales on their skin. All reptiles have a double-hinged jaw with multiple bones in the jaw and a single bone in each ear. Mammals give birth to their young, have mammary glands and have hair. They all have a single mandible or lower jaw that is hinged with a single joint on each side, and they all have three bones in each ear commonly called the hammer, anvil and stirrup. If the highly complex and integrated structures of mammals slowly and gradually evolved through mutations from the reptiles, the fossil record should show abundant evidence of the transformation.

Dr. Raup said that he knew nothing about the origin of mammals. He did not know of any evidence of this transition.

According to Dr. Patterson, some people say that the first mammals appeared in the Triassic, or they argue about Jurassic or Cretaceous and make up sequences for placental mammals, marsupials, etc. consistent with the story of evolution. But he could offer no fossil evidence that would support the stories. He acknowledged that the North American wolf and the marsupial Tasmanian wolf had comparable bone structures although they were assumed to have branched off from a common ancestor at the reptile stage.

When asked if he agreed that the first mammals were insectivores, Dr. Eldredge said that he had "no knowledge about that." Regarding the December 1976 *National Geographic* scenario on the origin of whales, he said that whales came out of some group of archaic ungulates.[10] He had written a paper several years ago and pointed out that in making up such accounts one was only limited by one's "own imagination and the credulity of the audience," but it was still "just a scenario, just a story." As science, he added, "It doesn't wash," In other words, since evolutionary scenarios are not part of testable science, the only limitation that restricts these authors is the gullibility level of the public.

Dr. Eldredge was then asked about these scenarios: "That is Dr. Patterson's point. He says in this letter (10 April 1979) to me that it is easy enough to make up stories, but he knows of not a single fossil or living transition.[11] You've been quoted in the papers as saying something similar." To this Dr. Eldredge answered, "Yes," and asked this author why the letter had been written to Dr. Patterson. The following reply was given: "Because the schools have been teaching some things that are misleading. When you dig into it you readily find this situation. Yet, teachers that I know of just present the whole thing as though it were a fact. We want to try to sort out the fiction from the science."

To this Dr. Eldredge said, "I want to teach you something

right now when you ask, is there not any part of evolution that is not a scenario?" He said that there were several things that people meant by evolution. There was evolution "supposed history," what he called the "actual sequence of events that took place in evolution." He slipped somewhat in calling it a supposition and then in the same sentence asserted that these supposed events actually took place. When asked if by this he meant viewing fossils, he replied that he meant comparing things that are alive today from an evolutionary point of view. In other words, he was saying that if you assumed that evolution actually occurred and then interpreted the similarities of organisms to be verification of this assumption, he called that "history." He said that the second aspect of evolution was the body of theory that purported to explain how it occurred, and the two should be kept separate.

He thought that some of the material about mechanisms could be scientifically treated — that it was open to a hypothetical deductive approach — but evolutionary history was an "entirely different kettle of fish." Scientists were trying to analyze that pattern. He said that there are some people who are fed up with this exact point about "imaginary stories" that have been written about the nature of the history of life. Dr. Eldredge said:

> I admit that an awful lot of that has gotten into the textbooks as though it were true. For instance, the most famous example still on exhibit downstairs (in the American Museum) is the exhibit on horse evolution prepared perhaps 50 years ago. That has been presented as literal truth in textbook after textbook. Now I think that that is lamentable, particularly because the people who propose these kinds of stories themselves may be aware of the speculative nature of some of the stuff. But by the time it filters down to the textbooks, we've got science as truth and we've got a problem.

So Dr. Eldredge said emphatically that some of the evolution stories printed in textbooks, like the one about the so-called horse series, are "lamentable."

The great differences between the reptilian and mammalian

masticatory apparatus as well as the differences between the ear mechanisms in these groups are major problems for evolutionists. All reptiles have seven bones in the lower jaw while all mammals, living or fossil, have a single jaw bone. Reptiles have a single bone in the inner ear while all mammals have three bones. Evolutionists contend that three reptile jaw bones on each side slowly migrated across the jaw joint up into the ear of the mammal, somehow replacing the single bone in the reptile ear. But there is no convincing scenario that can even be conceived for getting the jaw bones across the jaw joint.

A 1978 book, *Evolutionary Principles of the Mammalian Middle Ear*, is an authoritative treatment of the reptile-to-mammal transition relative to the problem of the ear bones.[12] The magazine *Evolution* carried a thorough review of this book. It said:

> These general statements about the evolution of the mammalian middle ear that appear are in the nature of proclamations. No methods are described which allow the reader to arrive with Fleischer at his "ancestral" middle ear, nor is the basis for the transformation series illustrated for the middle ear bones explained....Those searching for specific information useful in constructing phylogenies of mammalian taxa will be disappointed.[13]

Indeed, there are absolutely no fossils showing the migration of the jaw bones of the reptile up into the ear of the mammal.

Although the museum officials did not do so in their interviews, evolutionists frequently offer the so-called mammal-like reptiles as intermediates between the reptiles and mammals. There were hundreds of species of these creatures that were contemporaneous with many other early reptiles. They offer no solution for the reptile-to-mammal transition for they all appeared abruptly in the fossil record and even became extinct before the age of dinosaurs. A 1982 article in *New Scientist* magazine gave a good picture of the problem for evolutionists:

> Each species of mammal-like reptile that has been found appears suddenly in the fossil record and is not preceded by the species that is directly ancestral

to it. It disappears some time later, equally abruptly, without leaving a directly descended species...."[14]

The picture has not changed since George Gaylord Simpson wrote *Tempo and Mode in Evolution* in 1944, when he said:

This is true of all thirty-two orders of mammals ....The earliest and most primitive known members of every order already have the basic ordinal characters, and in no case is an approximately continuous sequence from one order to another known. In most cases the break is so sharp and the gap so large that the origin of the order is speculative and much disputed.[15]

Later Simpson confirmed that this absence of transitional forms was a systematic, universal phenomenon:

This regular absence of transitional forms is not confined to mammals, but is an almost universal phenomenon, as has long been noted by paleontologists. It is true of almost all classes of animals, both vertebrate and invertebrate...it is true of the classes, and of the major animal phyla, and it is apparently also true of analogous categories of plants.[16]

Roger Lewin wrote in *Science* magazine that the transition to the first mammal "is still an enigma."[17] But, then, this supposed transition should be no different than any of the others.

Origin of Horses

Not only was there general agreement among the museum officials about the questionable nature of some of the scenarios made up in an attempt to explain the lack of fossil or living evidence to support macroevolution, but there was also agreement on the so-called horse series. This series, commonly shown in school textbooks, starts with a four-toed *Hyracotherium,* passes through several three-toed creatures, and ends with a single-toed modern horse. Dr. Patterson agreed that it was not really a series at all. Dr. Raup said that, as more has been learned about the supposed evolution of the horse, more separate lineages have been recognized and it is far more complicated than early work indicated. He said that you do find lineages "on a small scale," but his museum's display omits the four-toed *Hyracotherium* completely and starts the display on horse evolution with a three-toed creature.

Horse evolution has been presented for many years in textbooks as a way to demonstrate how evolution has worked to originate a structure — the single toe. The first such series involving four steps was made in 1874, and the famous American Museum display on horse evolution, to which Dr. Eldredge referred, was made up in 1905. The 1964 book, *Atlas of Evolution*, by Sir Gavin de Beer, Director of the British Museum of Natural History, shows a highly detailed ladder of horse evolution.[18] A current textbook used for Regents biology in New York State, *Biology for You*, includes sketches of the horse series as the only illustration of fossils of intermediate forms between species.[19] But the people most familiar with the actual fossil evidence have a contrasting opinion about what the evidence indicates. Heribert-Nilsson says, "The family tree of the horse is beautiful and continuous only in the textbooks."[20] Here are some of the reasons.

Nowhere in the world are the fossils of the horse series found in successive strata. When they are found on the same continent, like in the John Day formation of Oregon, the three-toed and one-toed are found in the same geological horizon (stratum). In South America, the one-toed is even found below the three-toed creature.[21] And when other structures besides toes are considered, the picture does not look so impressive. For example, the four-toed *Hyracotherium* has 18 pairs of ribs, the next creature has 19, then there is a jump to 15, and finally back to 18 for *Equus*, the modern horse. The sequence requires arranging Old World and New World fossils side-by-side, and there is considerable dispute about the order in which they should be arranged. One specialist says, "The story depends to a large extent upon who is telling it and when the story is being told."

The four-toed *Hyracotherium* (now called *Eohippus*) does not look the least bit like a horse. When first found, it was classified as *Hyracotherium* because, skeletally, it was said to be identical to the rabbit-like hyrax or daman that is running around in the African bush today. *Eohippus* fossils have been found in surface strata alongside two types of modern horses, *Equus nevadensis* and *Equus occidentalis*.[22] The series shown in museum displays generally depicts an increase in size, and yet the range in size of living horses today from the tiny American miniature ponies to the enormous shires of England is as great as that found in the fossil record. It is no wonder that Dr. Eldredge called the textbook characterization of the horse series "lamentable."

When scientists speak in their offices or behind closed doors, they frequently make candid statements that sharply conflict with statements they make for public consumption before the media. For example, after Dr. Eldredge made the statement about the horse series being the best example of a lamentable imaginary story being presented as though it were literal truth, he contradicted himself. The morning of the beginning of the Seagraves' trial in California he was on a network television program. The host asked him to comment on the creationist claim that there were no examples of transitional forms to be found in the fossil record. Dr. Eldredge turned to the horse series display at the American Museum and stated that it was the best available example of a transitional sequence. On 14 February 1981 Sylvia Chase, host of the ABC Television program, 20/20, questioned him on this subject as follows:

Sylvia Chase: "Dr. Niles Eldredge, Curator of the Department of Invertebrates of the American Museum of Natural History, one of many scientists vigorously opposed to the creationists. I asked him for evidence (for evolution)."

Dr. Eldredge: "Ahh, the horse is a good example. Here's an effectively modern horse which is a million years old, but we can all recognize it as a horse. And as we go deeper in lower layers of rock, back further in time, we excavate successively more primitive horses. Here's one that is two million years old. They are becoming less and less obviously horselike till we get back 60 million years ago, and here is the ancestor of the horse which doesn't really look much like a horse. And the really interesting thing about this is that it is also the ancestor of the rhinoceros — or very close to the ancestor of the rhinoceros. So when the creationists tell us that we have no intermediates between major groups, we point to a creature like the dawn horse and say, 'Here we have 60 million years ago an exact intermediate between the horses and the rhinos.'[23] So in 1981, after joining the anticreationist campaign, Dr. Eldredge repeated a scenario for a nationwide audience that in 1979 he had called "lamentable."

Neck of the Giraffe

Charles Darwin devoted nearly a page in *The Origin* to a scenario that attempted to explain the origination of the neck of the giraffe. Although generally criticizing Lamarckism, in certain cases he accepted as an evolutionary mechanism the idea that offspring could inherit characteristics that the parents had acquired during their lifetime (Lamarckism). Using this idea, he speculated that the giraffe got its long neck by stretching higher and higher to reach leaves on trees as vegetation gradually dried up during a drought. There was more food on the highest branches and the least competition for them. The long neck was passed on to offspring. Today, however, the neck of the giraffe is commonly given as the classic example of how wrong Lamarck was.

It is not usually pointed out that the giraffe actually is an excellent example of how genetic principles restrict the amount of variation possible within mammals. Although a male giraffe may grow to about 20 feet tall, it has no more vertebrae in the neck than most other mammals, including man. The seven cervical vertebrae are simply elongated as are its legs.

It is speculated by neo-Darwinists that some ancestor of the giraffe gradually got longer and longer bones in the neck and legs over millions of years. If this were true, one might predict that there would either be fossils showing some of the intermediate forms or perhaps some living forms today with medium-sized necks. Absolutely no such intermediates have been found either among the fossil or living even-toed ungulates that would connect the giraffe with any other creature. Evolutionists cannot explain why the giraffe is the only four-legged creature with a really long neck and yet everything else in the world survived. Many short-necked animals of course existed side-by-side in the same locale as the giraffe. Darwin even mentioned this possible criticism in *The Origin* but tried to explain it away and ignore it. Furthermore it is not possible for evolutionists to make up a plausible scenario for the origination of either the giraffe's long neck or its complicated blood pressure regulating system. This amazing feature generates extremely high pressure to pump the blood up to the 20-foot-high brain and then quickly reduces the pressure to prevent brain damage when the animal bends down to take a drink. After over a century of the most intensive exploration for fossils, the world's museums cannot display a single intermediate form that would connect the giraffe with any other creature.

Origin of Elephants

Both the British Museum and American Museum of Natural History have displays that show the various types of elephants in a series, from one with short tusks and a long lower jaw to one with long tusks and a short lower jaw. But nowhere can be found an intermediate form that connects the elephants with a basically different creature. These institutions do display an elephant with tusks projecting from the lower jaw, but that doesn't solve the problem; it just creates another one. The first elephant in the series is clearly an elephant.

Origin of Primates

The first clue to the origin of the group of mammals in which man has been placed regards the orientation of the eyes. Man is classified as a primate along with apes, New World monkeys, Old World monkeys and prosimians (tarsiers, lemurs and tree shrews). All of the other primates have their eyes pointed forward, giving them binocular vision, however, the tree shrews have side vision as do the nonprimates such as dogs or deer. The popular scenario for the origin of primates speculates that, when animals climbed up into trees and started jumping from branch to branch, only those survived that had their eyes pointed forward so they could see better to catch the branches. Those with side vision were less fit in the trees. So museum displays show a lineage of the tree shrew followed by the tarsier with huge forward-facing eyes. But there is no fossil evidence of such a transition, for the shrews are distinct from the tarsiers. Furthermore, the reasonableness of the scenario seems questionable when it is given some thought. Squirrels have side vision, but they exhibit no less a capability of seeing the next branch when jumping about in the treetops than do the monkeys with binocular vision. At least they are not commonly known to miss and fall out of trees. The first shrews found as fossils are clearly shrews, and there is no fossil evidence connecting them with any creature with binocular vision.

The tarsiers have eyes located in the front of the skull, thus giving them binocular vision, but the first tarsiers are one-hundred percent tarsiers. The same is true with both the broad-nosed New World monkeys and the narrow-nosed Old World monkeys. The book, *Primates*, says that the origin of New World monkeys is obscure and even less is known about the Old World monkeys.[24] They appear abruptly in the fossil record as do the orangutans, chimpanzees, and gorillas.

In the Hall of Primates at the American Museum of Natural History, a mural fills one end of the display room. It was created by Dr. Eldredge to show the family tree of man and the other primates. A three-color code is used to indicate where the tree is based on actual fossils and where it is based on speculation. Portions of the tree shown in brown color represent reasonable guesses only. The tan portions are for "no fossils known" and the yellow sections represent actual fossils. It is especially significant that at every single fork in the tree, there is a brown and tan section indicating that it is based on guesses only without any actual fossil evidence.

Of the five natural history museum officials interviewed, Dr. David Pilbeam had the most expertise in the field of paleoanthropology (the study of fossil man) since he had worked specifically in this area for many years. He came to the attention of the scientific community as being an objective scientist when he wrote an article for *Human Nature* magazine, June 1978, entitled, "Rearranging Our Family Tree."[25] In it he reported that discoveries since 1976 had shaken his view of human origins and forced a change in ideas of man's early ancestors. His previous views were wrong about tool use replacing canine teeth, evidence for which was totally lacking. He did not believe any longer that he was likely to hit upon the true or correct story of the origin of man. He repeated a number of times that our theories have clearly reflected our current ideologies instead of the actual data. Too often they have reflected only what we expected of them.

In his interview, Dr. Pilbeam elaborated on the subjects he had discussed in his 1978 article. Currently, he was teaching a course that covered primates and was also doing field research in Africa and Pakistan. He was advising the Kenya government on the establishment of an international institute for the study of human origins. His office was near those of anthropologists Richard Leakey and his mother, Dr. Mary Leakey, in Nairobi, Kenya. He referred to several more recent publications, a review article in *Annual Reviews of Anthropology*, and several on his work in Pakistan.

Why had he changed his position on human origins? He said that it was not due to the discovery of only one particular specimen, but the recovery of various materials made him realize that his previous statements, which had been made so adamantly, were really based on very little evidence. He began to wonder, since they were based on so little evidence, why he had held them so strongly. It made him think about the nature of scientific thinking, and this precipitated a very profound change in his approach to analyzing data. He said that many of the statements made in the field of human origins had "very little to do with the real data and a great deal to do with unstated assumptions." He thought that this was true not only of his field but, "Much of what is said in other areas, I think, is also highly speculative."

Dr. Pilbeam said that there were two ways to look at evolutionary theory: the punctuated way and the gradual way. Before the punctuated equilibria theory came along, scientists said emphatically that there was only one way. Dr. Pilbeam thought that it would be very difficult to tell for most mammal groups which alternative was correct, but he thought that some people who disagreed with punctuated equilibria theory did so on philosophical rather than empirical grounds. He emphasized that this was why he had made such a point in his 1978 article that one's preconceived notions shape the way one perceives data.

Dr. Patterson agreed about the lack of fossil evidence connecting man with a lower primate. In answer to the question, "What do you think of the Australopithecines as man's ancestors?," Dr. Patterson replied, "There is no way of knowing whether they are the ancestors to anything or not."

So, the museum officials who were in an excellent position to know about the fossil evidence relating to the origin of man had very little to say about the subject. If any actual fossil evidence existed showing how man could be connected with any other primate group, it is unlikely that they would have kept silent about it.

Richard Leakey summed up the situation on the final Walter Cronkite *Universe* program. He said that if he were going to draw a family tree for man, he would just draw a huge question mark. He said that the fossil evidence was too scanty for us to possibly know man's evolutionary origin, and he did not think we were ever going to know it.

William R. Fix has written a book, *The Bone Peddlers* (1984), in which he examined in great detail what the most prominent evolutionary paleoanthropologists have said about each of the various fossils that have been claimed to show evidence of man's ancestry. He showed how further studies and more recent discoveries have eliminated each of man's supposed apelike ancestors from his family tree. He wrote:

> The fossil record pertaining to man is still so sparsely known that those who insist on positive declarations can do nothing more than jump from one hazardous surmise to another and hope that the next dramatic discovery does not make them utter fools.... Clearly, some people refuse to learn from this. As we have seen, there are numerous scientists and popularizers today who have the temerity to tell us that there is 'no doubt' how man originated. If only they had the evidence....
>
> I have gone to some trouble to show that there are formidable objections to all the subhuman and

near-human species that have been proposed as
ancestors.[26]

Mr. Fix expresses his preference for evolution theory over
that of creation, but he insists that his fellow evolutionists
have been playing loosely with the rules of science and have
conveniently overlooked the contradictory evidence:

> So, when it comes to the fossil record, or any
> other body of evidence, for the sake of the good
> cause they accentuate the supportive data and
> ignore or minimize as far as possible the contrary
> indications.[27]

Origin of Insects

Is there any indication of a gradual origin of insects? Dr.
Raup gave the most vivid description of the fossil evidence on
insects. He said, "This whole question of intermediates I
think is questionable. For example, the insect life in the Carboniferous is wonderful. The insects were well out in hundreds
of species. My point is that during the Cretaceous there were
65 to 75 million years with virtually no insect fossils." The
Cretaceous Period, when dinosaurs are supposed to have
flourished, is dated at about 100 million years after the flying
insects abruptly appeared in the coal beds of the Carboniferous Period. He said that only a handful of specimens
of insects have been found in the Cretaceous. When asked to
explain this fact he said that it was just "bad luck." But when
it was suggested that it might be due to the way the strata and
fossils were deposited, he responded that he would certainly
agree.

Are There Any Documented Transitional Fossils?

None of the five museum officials could offer a single
example of a transitional series of fossilized organisms that
would document the transformation of one basically different
type to another. Dr. Eldredge said that the categories of
families and above could not be connected while Dr. Raup said
that a dozen or so large groups could not be connected with
each other. But Dr. Patterson spoke most freely about the
absence of transitional forms.

Before interviewing Dr. Patterson, the author read his book, *Evolution*, which he had written for the British Museum of Natural History.[28] In it he had solicited comments from readers about the book's contents and a letter was written to Dr. Patterson asking why he did not put a single photograph of a transitional fossil in his book. On 10 April 1979 he replied to the author in a most candid letter as follows:

...I fully agree with your comments on the lack of direct illustration of evolutionary transitions in my book. If I knew of any, fossil or living, I would certainly have included them. You suggest that an artist should be used to visualise such transformations, but where would he get the information from? I could not, honestly, provide it, and if I were to leave it to artistic licence, would that not mislead the reader?

I wrote the text of my book four years ago. If I were to write it now, I think the book would be rather different. Gradualism is a concept I believe in, not just because of Darwin's authority, but because my understanding of genetics seems to demand it. Yet Gould and the American Museum people are hard to contradict when they say there are no transitional fossils. As a palaeontologist myself, I am much occupied with the philosophical problems of identifying ancestral forms in the fossil record. You say that I should at least 'show a photo of the fossil from which each type of organism was derived.' I will lay it on the line — there is not one such fossil for which one could make a watertight argument. The reason is that statements about ancestry and descent are not applicable in the fossil record. Is *Archaeopteryx* the ancestor of all birds? Perhaps yes, perhaps no: there is no way of answering the question. It is easy enough to make up stories of how one form gave rise to another, and to find reasons why the stages should be favoured by natural selection. But such stories are not part of science, for there is no way of putting them to the test.

So, much as I should like to oblige you by jumping
to the defence of gradualism, and fleshing out the
transitions between the major types of animals and
plants, I find myself a bit short of the intellectual
justification necessary for the job. . . .[29]

In his interview several months later, Dr. Patterson was
asked to elaborate, "You stated in your letter that there are
no transitions. Do you know of any good ones?" He replied,
"No, I don't, not that I would try to support. No." Throughout
the interview he denied having transitional fossil candidates
for each specific gap between the major different groups. He
said that there are kinds of change in forms taken in isolation
but there are none of these sequences that people like to build
up. Putting it as a question, he said, "If you ask, 'What is the
evidence for continuity?' you would have to say, 'There isn't
any in the fossils of animals and man. The connection between them is in the mind.'"

Did he "know of any documented evolution going on today
in the macro sense where we're looking for a new structure that
previously did not exist — like an arm forming?" He answered,
"No, not of an arm forming, not in the macro sense." Then he
was asked, "Then you know of no structure that you could
classify as developing and not fully functional?" Reply: "No."
It was noted that some authors are claiming that there is no real
evolution going on today other than minor variations like the
shift in coloration in moths. He said that he would have to
agree; he did not know of any either. What did he see as the
biggest problem with the concept of evolution? He said that it
was a philosophical problem. People seem to find the evidence they are looking for. He did not think it was possible to
find the answer to origins in science: "There are solutions to
problems in science but I don't think this is science we are talking about, I think it's history." With this perceptive statement
there can be no rational argument.

Such devastating statements do not, however, seem to affect
the faith of hard-line evolutionists. They just make up stories
to explain them away. For example, philosophy professor
Philip Kitcher, a well-known apologist for evolution-only
teaching, gave this attempted explanation for Dr. Patterson's

letter in a television debate with the author 3 May 1984. The host asked the evolutionists, "The fact that there are no transitional fossils at the British Museum — why would this fellow write this letter?"

Dr. Kitcher replied:

> Dr. Patterson, when he wrote that letter in 1979, he wrote that letter in complete ignorance of the political situation in the USA. He thought that he was writing a letter to a fellow professional scientist...." When people like Dr. Patterson have disagreements with their professional colleagues, these things are torn out of context by creation scientists."

Thus, Dr. Kicher tried to discount Dr. Patterson's devastating statements in his letter by inferring that he would not have been so truthful if he had known of the great public controversy in the USA over how theories on origins should be taught. This aspersion on Dr. Patterson's character is without foundation for Dr. Patterson repeated the same points and made even stronger statements in his interview with the author several months later. This was after he had been told of the situation in public education in the USA and a month earlier had been given two creation-science books to read. They were: *Evolution? The Fossils Say No!* by Gish[30] and *The Creation/Evolution Controversy* by Wysong.[31] In the interview he explicitly said that he knew of no transitional fossils and that evolution was based on faith alone.

Did Dr. Fisher know of any transitional forms between the higher taxa? He replied, "Intermediates within families and even within orders, but not between phyla. Nor do I think you will ever find any between phyla." Why? His only answer was the standard one — the imperfection of the fossil record. "You can either say that there are no transitional forms, or you can say that because of the vagaries of preservation, only one in ten million of this particular species was ever preserved." That would add up to a heap of fish considering the billions that were preserved in the Lompoc formation alone! One is forced into the most ridiculous positions when making up stories to explain why the fossil record falsifies the theory of common-ancestry evolution.

In his 1979 interview with the author, Dr. Eldredge was much more candid about the lack of ancestors in the fossil record. He said, "I've got problems with ancestors, too. That's why when I work with the history of life I'm with guys like Patterson." He said that all he tried to do was chart the nested sets of resemblances and arrive at the least objectionable sort of theory about how things were related in a general sort of way. He said that he made "no definite statements about who was ancestral to whom." Then in 1981 he repeated a scenario for a nationwide audience that in 1979 he had called "lamentable," and he claimed that *Eohippus* was "an exact intermediate" between the horses and the rhinos.

He did say in 1979 that when you were working at the species level you could find ancestors and descendants. But when asked, "Isn't it more than at the species level?" he responded, "No, just among species, that's all." It was pointed out that some people say that maybe families can be connected and he replied, "They are wrong. How can a family evolve?" He said that what we think we know about evolutionary mechanisms is that natural selection, working on natural variation within species, brings about the origin of new species which bud off from the old communities. You take these lineages and put them together in larger and larger groups but those groups do not have the same ecological existence that species have. So, he said that his position and that of others was that "species are real units in nature." He said, "The genera, families, etc., even if they are smaller lineages, don't exist in the same sense as a species. They only evolve as their component species do. Therefore, the idea of a family being ancestral to another family is illogical. It never happens."

This is a rather confusing explanation of why there are no transitional forms to be found either among the living or fossilized organisms. If every living organism had an ancestry that consisted of an unbroken lineage connected to a single-celled organism, it should make no difference whatsoever if man has decided to call the various stages along the way by different names. Just as the organisms within a species can be connected, so should the different species, genera, families, orders, classes, and kingdoms be shown to be connected. That is a specific prediction that obviously should be made from the theory of common-ancestry evolution if it were a truly scientific theory. If all life had a common ancestor, how could it be "illogical" for one family to be ancestral to another family? Every organism in the continuum between a single cell and man is a member of one of the various families. Webster's dictionary says that "ancestral" means "derived from an ancestor." Since the theory of evolution, as Dr. Eldredge speaks of it, holds that all life came from a common ancestor, there is no conceivable way that the English language could be distorted to permit one to correctly state that no family could be ancestral to another family. Certainly some lower family should be ancestral to every higher family if evolution actually occurred.

The author made the following reply to this statement by Dr. Eldredge: "Somehow the family that dogs or cows are in had to arise. You think there are transitions at the species level, but do you know of any at a higher level? That is really what it is all about when you get down to it. Where did even a vertebrate come from? That would be easy to recognize."

Dr. Eldredge replied that if you took cats and dogs, the closest that he would ever put it was that you had two separate families and the closest relative was some other one like, say, hyenas. Hyenas (Hyaenidae) and cats (Felidae) are the closest relatives because they might share some similarities that are not shared with any other group. He concluded, "Now you might suspect that you have the ancestor by this line of reasoning." He also used the example of the supposed human ancestor, *Australopithecus africanus*. The skull of that was very difficult to assess for he had tried and tried when he was working as an anthropologist to find a particular feature that would have allowed him to say that it shared a specialized resemblance with, say, *Australopithecus robustus* as opposed to *Homo habilis*. He said that some people say, "Ah ha! It's an ancestor." But he said that he did not know if it were an ancestor or not. He said, "There is no way to really come to grips with it logically."

Dr. Eldredge should have stated that there was no logical way to harmonize the scientific evidence with the theory of common-ancestry evolution since no connections between any basically different groups of organisms could be documented with fossils. He did not mean that it would be impossible to connect families if evolution were true. He meant that there was no way to connect them using either fossil or living evidence.

What did Darwin say about the lack of transitional forms in the fossil record? This lack actually gave him great concern, and he wrote an entire chapter in *The Origin* about it. Generally, he explained the absence away with the argument that these forms just were not fortunate enough to have become fossilized, and there had not been enough geological research done by 1859. For some reason, Gillespie did not think this was explaining away the evidence when he wrote, "Darwin's analysis of the fossil record then was not an ad hoc 'explaining away' of an embarrassing absence of evidence, but a revealing of how unreasonable it was to demand that evidence because of the nature of geological processes and the youth of paleontological science."[32] And later he explained, "As shown, the absence of transitional forms in the fossil record had long been one of the strongest arguments against transmutation (common ancestry). In the 1861 edition of *The Origin*, Darwin enjoyed reporting that the 'assertion' that 'geology has yielded no linking forms...is entirely erroneous.' "[33] It is strange that, after over a century of searching for the linking forms, the world's greatest fossil museums have not been able to find them, unless perhaps, they do not exist.

Origin of Plants

The origin of plants appears to be a complete mystery to evolutionists. It is difficult to find even a postulated family tree of plant life. Dr. Patterson said that he had seen a lot published on the origin of plants, "Although I would agree that they are not convincing."

Dr. E.J.H. Corner of the Cambridge University botany school made a candid evaluation of the knowledge about plant evolution: "Much evidence can be adduced in favor of the theory of evolution — from biology, biogeography and paleontology, but I still think that to the unprejudiced, the fossil record of plants is in favor of special creation."[34]

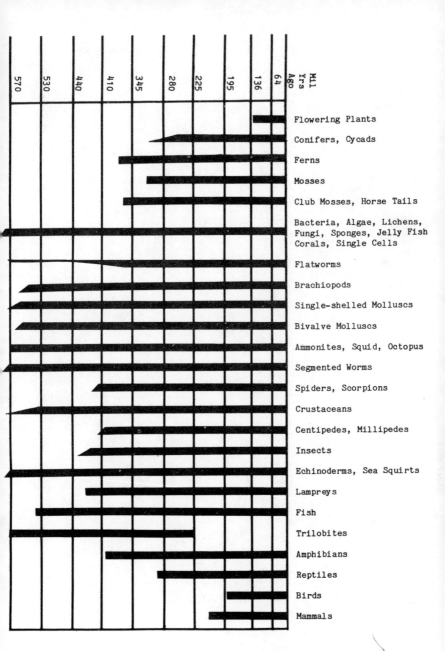

Figure 5. The actual fossil record shows the abrupt appearance and extinction of basic different life forms with no intermediate forms connecting them. It depicts sudden appearance and stasis.

P.150

In the book *The Evolution of Life*, E.C. Olson said: "A third fundamental aspect of the record is somewhat different. Many new groups of plants and animals suddenly appear, apparently without any close ancestors. Most major groups of organisms — phyla, subphyla, and even classes — have appeared in this way."[35] He said that this is usually explained away by the argument that the fossil record did not record the intermediates, but, "Some paleontologists disagree and believe that these events tell a story not in accord with the theory and not seen among living organisms."[36]

The End of Gradualism

Today many scientists are abandoning gradualistic evolution because of two undeniable characteristics of the fossil record: the abrupt appearance of new basic types of organisms followed by little or no change. The emerging paleontological picture is shown in Figure 5 which is based on a similar diagram recently published in BBC's *Life on Earth*[37] and *Evolution from Space*[38] by Fred Hoyle and Chandra Wickramasinghe.

Chapter 5

More Problems Than Solutions

What Is Punctuated Equilibria?

Ever since the time of Charles Darwin, people have pointed to the abrupt appearance of the various forms of life in the fossil record as being in conflict with the idea that all life gradually and slowly evolved from a common ancestor. They have argued that any realistic theory on origins should account for this evidence. Darwin talked extensively about this problem in *The Origin*: "Mr. Mivart is further inclined to believe, and some naturalists agree with him, that new species manifest themselves 'with suddenness and by modifications appearing at once.'" Of course, Darwin disagreed with this since he was firmly convinced of gradualism. He concluded: "My reasons for doubting whether natural species have changed as abruptly as have occasionally domestic races, and for entirely disbelieving that they have changed in the wonderful manner indicated by Mr. Mivart, are as follows."[1]

At the turn of the century, well-known geneticist pioneer Hugo De Vries talked about the saltation of new species from time to time. Saltation means a sudden or abrupt change, a jump or leap. Through the years, others, like Europe's top paleontologist, O.H. Schindewolf, felt that evolution had proceeded by sudden jumps. In the 1930s he proposed that a reptile laid an egg and hatched out a full-fledged bird as an explanation of the reptile-to-bird gap. Then in 1940, world-famous geneticist from Berkeley, California, Dr. Richard

Goldschmidt, made the concept famous with his book *The Material Basis for Evolution*.[2] He noted that paleontologists had searched for a hundred years since the time of Darwin for transitional forms in the fossil record without finding any. Obviously, none were ever going to be found, and if evolutionists were going to keep the faith, they needed a new theory. So he proposed the "hopeful monster theory." He said that every now and then a two-legged sheep or a two-headed turtle was born. They were all monsters and died but, hopefully, over enough time, there might be a good one which would survive. He said that every time there was a gap in the fossil record, a monster had been born. For example, he said that he agreed with Schindewolf's suggestion that the first bird had hatched from the egg of a reptile.

Needless to say, Goldschmidt's hopeful monster theory was met with much derision. Critics said that there was not a shred of evidence to support his theory. He responded that this was unfair criticism because neither was there a shred of evidence for slow and gradual evolution. No one paid much attention to Goldschmidt because in the 1940s there was much excitement and hopeful anticipation over the new Darwinism that Simpson, Mayr, Dobzhansky, and others were writing volumes about. Then came the so-called creation science movement of the 1950s and 1960s, which focused much public attention on the complete lack of intermediate forms in both the fossil record and living organisms. An alternative theory to gradualism was badly needed, for the continued absence of transitional forms was beginning to cause great embarrassment in the evolutionist camp.

A graduate student working with Bolivian trilobites was the one to propose the theory that sparked a revolution. Niles Eldredge said that in 1972 he discovered some features in the fossil record that just did not fit the idea of slow and gradual evolution. He enlisted the assistance of Stephen Jay Gould of Harvard and introduced the world to the theory they called punctuated equilibria. Here is how Gould described this event in an article in *Discover* magazine, May 1981:

> In 1972 my colleague Niles Eldredge and I developed the theory of punctuated equilibrium. We

argued that two outstanding facts of the fossil
record — geologically 'sudden' origin of new species
and failure to change thereafter (stasis) — reflect
the predictions of (this new) evolutionary theory,
not the imperfections of the fossil record.[3]

He contended that the lack of intermediate forms in the
fossil record could not continue to be explained away with
stories about the unlikelihood of anything but the terminal
forms with completed organs being fossilized. This absence of
intermediates he called a trend: "Trends, we argued, cannot
be attributed to gradual transformation within lineages, but
must arise from the differential success of certain kinds of
species."[4] It was more like climbing stairs than rolling up an
incline.

At a convention of science writers 19 November 1978 in
Gatlinburg, Tennessee, Dr. Eldredge was quoted by the *Los
Angeles Times* as saying that if life had evolved into the
wondrous profusion of creatures little by little, then there
should be some fossiliferous record of those changes. The
report said:

But no one has found any such in-between
creatures. This was long chalked up to 'gaps' in the
fossil records, gaps that proponents of gradualism
confidently expected to fill in someday when rock
strata of the proper antiquity were eventually
located. But all of the fossil evidence to date has
failed to turn up any such missing links, Eldredge
said and there is a growing conviction among many
scientists that these transitional forms never existed.
And if this is so, then the gradualist view of evolution is an inaccurate portrayal of how life developed.[5]

Dr. Eldredge said that if the conventional picture were true,
paleontologists should find a slow, gradual change in fossils.
Instead, he said, the fossil record is quite different. It shows the
"sudden appearance" of species that exist almost unchanged
for several thousand years. He said that this picture holds true
for human evolution also. The fossil record shows a jump to
Neanderthal man and another jump to *Homo sapiens*. This

new theory says the missing links should never be found because they never existed. Eldredge said that his theory of punctuated equilibria could be wiped out if a single series of intermediates was found in the fossil record. But no such series has been found. (Note that the official name of the theory uses the plural form, "equilibria," although even Stephen Gould often incorrectly uses it in the singular, "equilibrium.")

Dr. Raup seemed to think that there was a general revolution going on in evolutionary thinking. In fact he wrote a section for a 1980 yearbook for the *World Book Encyclopedia* that was entitled *Revolution in Evolution*.[6] In his 1979 interview, he had this to say about hopeful monsters and punctuated equilibria:

> All of the authors of the neo-Darwinian theory which they formulated back in the thirties and forties are losing their influence. They are getting old and dying off. I predict that that whole concept will be thrown out in the next ten years and a new theory will be devised to take its place. A new wave of thinking is sweeping the field.

What will be the new theory? Dr. Raup confessed, "I have no idea."

Here is what Dr. Patterson thought of punctuated equilibria:

> Well, it seems to me that they have accepted that the fossil record doesn't give them the support they would value so they searched around to find another model and found one. The support they get for that model comes from geneticists and population biologists who have trouble imagining how a large population could split. So they say it doesn't have to happen that way. A population was isolated by a catastrophe of some sort. Once you start applying that reasoning to the fossil record, you are doing what these people (creationists) are saying you are doing. When you haven't got the evidence, you make up a story that will fit the lack of evidence.

Norman Macbeth was a bit stronger in his evaluation of the punctuationalist idea. In an interview with the author on 29

May 1982 he expounded his assessment. He felt that Eldredge and Gould came out with their version of it partly in response to his 1971 book *Darwin Retried*.[7] He first commented about Goldschmidt's version of the theory:

> A wild suggestion to meet a glaring need. In 1940, Goldschmidt promoted an idea of evolution that has come to be known as the hopeful monster theory. He noted in desperation that since no one could find any mechanism that was operating slowly and steadily in the Darwinian sense, it seemed impossible to explain evolution on the basis of accumulating tiny steps. He was thus driven to the idea that changes occurred in large and very sudden steps. He said there were systemic mutations which caused a complete shake-up. The products were usually monsters like two-legged sheep. They couldn't survive but hopefully if there were enough of them, you might get a good one, hence the label Hopeful Monster theory. Critics pointed out that with such a large change occurring suddenly the new form would find it very difficult to find an equally monstrous partner with which to reproduce.

Why had Macbeth been calling hopeful monsters "the hypothesis of despair?"

> Because Goldschmidt saw macroevolution as the big problem and found no answer to it in neo-Darwinism. In other words, the central question is the origination of new species with new structures and features. Gradual minute changes never seem to be the answer since they only change something that is already in existence. Since my book came out ten years ago, there has been a great revival of interest in Goldschmidt's idea. Many people, like Gould, are now saying Goldschmidt was on the right track, although he never produced a mechanism that you could document. They say it did happen that way in sudden large jumps without cumulating insensible changes, as Darwin called them. Goldschmidt recognized that he was, to some extent, pipe

dreaming, but he felt it necessary to pipe dream because the synthetic theory offered nothing. He was driven to this because the fossil record offered no evidence of gradual change. I sympathize with Goldschmidt personally, but I do not espouse the idea of a hopeful monster because, as any fool can see, it is extremely difficult to document, in fact, impossible. This is not a scientific theory; it is only a statement that shows we are in such terrible shape that we have to admit that the changes must have been on the order of a miracle.

Question: "What happened at the meeting in the Chicago Field Museum on Natural History in October 1980 where 160 scientists met to discuss macroevolution? Did most of them support some form of punctuated equilibria as *Newsweek* magazine reported?"[8] To this Macbeth replied:

There were various kinds of scientists assembled there for three or four days to discuss the problems of macroevolution, and they got absolutely nowhere. The impression I got from two or three people who attended it was one of spectacular bankruptcy. They had no theory whatsoever to explain macroevolution. It is still in the condition it was in Goldschmidt's time with Gould and others now recognizing it. They have nothing to offer except the faint hope that in epigenesis they may someday find something.

Paleobiologist Steven Stanley, a professor at Johns Hopkins University, is one of the most outspoken proponents of punctuated equilibria theory. In 1979 he authored the book, *Macroevolution: Pattern and Process* which attacked gradualism and attempted to defend the punctuationalist view of evolution.[9] Then in June 1982, he wrote an update on this thesis in *Johns Hopkins Magazine* entitled, "The New Evolution." In it he summarized in very strong terms the case against the gradualistic theory of evolution.[10]

First, he showed how Charles Darwin was a gradualist, quoting him from *The Origin*:

It may be said metaphorically that natural selection is daily and hourly scrutinizing, throughout the world, every variation, even the slightest; rejecting that which is bad, preserving and adding up all that is good; silently and insensibly working, whenever and wherever opportunity offers, at the improvement of each organic being in relation to its organic and inorganic condition of life. We see nothing of these slow changes in progress, until the hand of time has marked the long lapse of ages. . . .

Stanley wrote that, although this gradualistic view of evolution had ruled evolutionary thought for over a century, he took issue with it:

Having carefully scrutinized data from the fossil record during the past decade, however, I have demonstrated a biological stability for species of animals and plants that I think would have shocked Darwin. Certainly it has jolted many modern evolutionists.

He gave examples of various species that remained stable for millions of years such as tiny foraminifera, molluscs, beetles, mammals, mosses and higher plants. He said that some biologists had doubted the veracity of this evidence, suggesting that fossil remains provided too imperfect a picture of the history of life, but, "This, I would argue, is an unfair charge."

His argument focuses on beetles since their genitalia are so specialized. Beetle genitalia are so uniquely constructed that they enable individual beetles to mate exclusively with members of their own species. This permits scientists to identify members of the many thousands of beetle species, and it so happens that beetle genitalia are durable structures that preserve well as fossils, thus providing reliable information on the antiquity and stability of the species. He argued that since there was no change in the key aspects of body form that differentiate species, it is almost a certainty that the species underwent no evolution save for a bit of "fine tuning."

Professor Stanley acknowledged that at times we might fail to distinguish between closely similar species within genera, "but errors of this sort have no bearing on the question at hand. Even if evolution does occasionally occur by a tiny step, such a small change cannot help explain the major shifts seen elsewhere." He reasonably argues, "To explain large-scale evolution, we need to look at large-scale evolution."

Large volumes of fossil data now available from all over the world (not available in Darwin's time) permit us to make these generalizations according to Stanley:

> Once established, an average species of animal or plant will not change enough to be regarded as a new species, even after surviving for something like a hundred thousand, or a million, or even ten million generations. . . . Something tends to prevent the wholesale restructuring of a species, once it has become well established on earth.

> The stability of species is all the more remarkable when we observe that dramatically new kinds of animals and plants have indeed appeared in very little geological time.

In order to defend the pure assumption that life had evolved from a common ancestor in spite of a total lack of supportive fossil evidence, Stanley offered the rapid-change-within-small-populations proposition. He thought that this would account for the fact that macroevolution was not recorded in the fossils and "we are forced to conclude that most evolution has occurred rapidly within small populations and in local areas. . . ."

He admitted that there was no known mechanism for this sudden jump or major restructuring of life supposition: "At present, we have no certain answer." Apparently it has not occurred to Professor Stanley that he is trying to prop up the theory of common-ancestry evolution which has been refuted by the direct fossil evidence and it is time to deposit it in the trash can.

The theory of punctuated equilibria is causing much turmoil among evolutionists. They know that there is no actual mechanism that would explain large rapid jumps from one species to another, and yet they also know the fossil record does not support gradualism. They are left on the horns of a dilemma. Some thus try to take the middle-of-the-road position and claim that both gradualism and punctuated equilibria are correct explanations. Gould does not see it that way, however.

Stephen Jay Gould on Problems with Gradualism

At a conference at Hobart College on 14 February 1980 to honor Mary Leakey, Dr. Gould elaborated on his theories about evolution.[11] First, he affirmed that the essence of the evolutionary process was selection leading to adaptation. The so-called "modern synthesis," which came to be accepted particularly after Dobzhansky's 1937 book *Genetics and the Origin of Species,*[12] and Simpson's 1944 book, *Tempo and Mode of Evolution*, embraced "mutation, selection and gradual accumulation."[13] Gould said that he had been beguiled as a graduate student in the mid-1960s with the notion that, by studying the processes governing populations of *Drosophila* fruit flies in bottles, you could explain everything that occurred over millions of years in evolution and that slow, gradual sequential substitution of genes within local populations, all leading to adaptations, is the essence of the evolutionary process at all levels. He said that he had since watched the modern synthesis gradually come apart. If Ernst Mayr's characterization of it were accurate, "then the theory as a general proposition is no longer adequate to explain evolution in spite of its persistence in textbook orthodoxy." He said that a typical 900-page textbook on biology would contain only two paragraphs on macroevolution "because there is no theory of macroevolution in the modern synthesis...there is no theory because everything can be extrapolated out of what happens in local populations, so two paragraphs is fine."

Dr. Gould emphasized the random nature of the process of change. He said:

> The point is that Darwinism holds to this very basis, that random factors enter only into the production of raw material. That's the whole point. We've got a theory that selection controls the direction of variation in raw materials only. That's what's random, and it's the deterministic processes of selection that produce change and direction. So, in fact, random factors produce change. That is not what Darwin contended as I understand it.

He disputed the whole idea that minor variations such as
in the coloration in moths could be extrapolated to explain
the major changes in macroevolution. It is an elegant story,
but the question is, "is that a model for everything else?" New
models of evolution, he said, were at variance with the synthetic proposition that speciation is merely an extension of
microevolution within local populations. He argued that you
cannot extrapolate the evolutionary trend from the level of
change within local populations.

The gaps in the fossil record, he insisted, could not be
explained away with the excuse that the fossil deposition
process just somehow skipped recording the intermediate
stages. Dr. Gould said:

> The fossil record is full of gaps and discontin-
> uities, but they are all attributed to the notorious
> imperfection of the fossil record. The fossil record is
> imperfect, but I think that is not an adequate
> explanation...one thing it does show that cannot
> be attributed to its imperfection is that most species
> don't change....They may get a little bigger or
> bumpier but they remain the same species and that's
> not due to imperfection and gaps but stasis. And yet
> this remarkable stasis has generally been ignored as
> no data. If they don't change, it's not evolution so
> you don't talk about it.

Actually, he should have said that lack of change *is* stasis,
not due to stasis.

Dr. Gould argued that changes were abrupt, not gradual.
For example, in human evolution, he said, "There is no evidence that the increase in size of the human brain is one of these
slow and steady, accumulative, adaptive, sequential,
advantageous changes." What role do mutations play in
speciation? Dr. Gould answered:

> A mutation doesn't produce major new raw
> material. You don't make a new species by mutating
> the species....That's a common idea people have;
> that evolution is due to random mutations. A muta-
> tion is NOT the cause of evolutionary change.
> Something else than natural selection brings about

species at new levels, trends and direction.

During the question-and-answer session following his Hobart lecture, Dr. Gould was asked if there was not stratigraphic evidence indicating gradualism? He emphasized his answer with a burst of profanity and a slap of his fist on the table:

> The fundamental reason why a lot of paleontologists don't care much for gradualism is because the fossil record doesn't show gradual change and every paleontologist has known that ever since Cuvier. If you want to get around that you have to invoke the imperfection of the fossil record. Every paleontologist knows that most species, most species, don't change. That's bothersome if you are trained to believe that evolution ought to be gradual. In fact it virtually precludes your studying the very process you went into the school to study. Again, because you don't see it, that brings terrible distress.

Unfortunately, the vast majority of students have not spent a lifetime searching for transitional forms in the fossil record as Dr. Gould has done and they are not aware that there is none. Frank statements like these by Dr. Gould are censored for school materials. Textbooks frequently contain dogmatic statements about how well the fossil record documents evolution, so instead of experiencing "terrible distress," students develop a comforting faith that there must be some good evidence somewhere that would substantiate common-ancestry evolution. They are still indoctrinated with the idea that mutations *do* "produce major new raw material" and that mutations thus provide the ultimate creative source for the entire biosphere.

Needless to say, Stephen Gould's statements have caused great consternation among the faithful followers of Charles Darwin who expend great effort in attempting to downplay Gould's embarrassing statements about the triviality of natural selection as a major explanation for the generation of basically new genetic information. For example, *Nature* magazine, 10 May 1984, reported on lectures Gould had just given at Cambridge University: "It is therefore a relief to be able to report that...Gould and eight invited discussants concluded that by and large, Darwin...got it right."[14] The words "by and large" certainly must allow for a huge margin of error unless Gould is wrong about the lack of evidence for gradualism.

Social Implications of Punctuational Theories

Some evolutionists reject the punctuationalist version of evolution for sociological reasons, contending that it is a philosophy growing out of the revolutionary concept of Marxism. Dr. Beverly Halstead of Reading University in England has expressed this objection in print several times. Although, to an outsider, there might appear to be a rather tenuous connection, the claim does have some substance if statements by its current champions have any relevance. Gould and Eldredge explicitly made the association in an article about punctuated equilibria in *Paleobiology* magazine:

> Alternative conceptions of change have respectable pedigrees in philosophy. Hegel's dialectical laws, translated into a materialist context, have become the official "state philosophy" of many socialist nations. These laws of change are explicitly punctuational, as befits a theory of revolutionary transformation in human society.

They apparently feel that Marxism is a viable politicial system which they prefer:

> In the light of this official philosophy, it is not at all surprising that a punctuational view of speciation, much like our own, but devoid (so far as we can tell) of references to synthetic evolutionary theory and the allopatric model, has long been favored by many Russian paleontologists. It may also not be irrelevant to our personal preferences that one of us learned his Marxism, literally, at his daddy's knee.[15]

It is interesting that Gould has occasionally tried to give the impression that he objected to being called a Marxist, but yet has never denied being one. In fact, at least once under oath

in a court deposition for the trial regarding the constitution-
ality of the Louisiana Balanced Treatment Law, he acknowledged that he was a Marxist.

In "The Darwin Debate," *Marxism Today*, Young wrote:

> Aspects of evolutionism are perfectly consistent
> with Marxism. The explanation of the origins of
> humankind and of mind by purely natural forces
> was, and remains, as welcome to Marxists as to any
> other secularists. The sources of value and respon-
> sibility are not to be found in a separate mental
> realm or in an immortal soul, much less in the
> inspired words of the Bible.[16]

Theodosius Dobzhansky was one of the authors of the neo-
Darwinian synthetic theory, which temporarily salvaged
Darwinism in the 1930s when it was practically dead. He was
told how, when the communists overthrew the Czarist government and took control in Russia in 1917, they needed a
materialistic basis for their world system. They recognized
evolution as the solution to the problem, accepting it as their
official explanation of dialectical materialism. They virtually
raised Charles Darwin to sainthood.

Just before his death, Dobzhansky gave a paper at a 1974
conference organized to review the history and status of the
evolutionary synthesis. The papers given at this conference
were published in a book by Ernst Mayr and William Provine,
The Evolutionary Synthesis. In Dobzhansky's paper, "The
Birth of the Genetic Theory of Evolution in the Soviet Union
in the 1920s," he gave a historical sketch of evolution theory
in Russia and showed how it formed the basis for the new
communist political movement which was germinating there:

> When Darwin's *On the Origin of Species* was
> published in 1859, Russia was entering a period of
> political reforms and a ground swell of radicalism
> among its intelligentsia. The coincidence was for-
> tuitous, but it left an impress on the intellectual
> tradition. Evolution was accepted not only as a
> scientific theory but also as a part of the liberal
> world view...standard bearers of the radical youth
> proclaimed that a valid personal philosophy must
> rest on a solid base of natural science, and evolu-

tion was a pivotal part of that.[17]

He said that although some scientists had some reservations about certain parts of Darwin's theory, they still "accepted evolution as part of the new gospel." The scientific discussion of the problem was taken over by Marxist philosophers in the 1920s and early 1930s. At that time the Timiriazev Institute was working on "the study and propaganda of the scientific foundations of dialectical materialism." He wrote, "The debates among the high priests of dialectics were often impassioned but inconclusive. Both Lamarckians and Darwinians claimed to be faithful dialecticians." Dialectical materialism is the theory, advanced by Marx and Engles, that there is a continuous transformation of matter and an interconnectedness of things implying social transformation through socialism toward a classless society.

When Dobzhansky left Russia on December 4, 1927, he brought with him the major tenets of what later was to be called "neo-Darwinism" or the "modern synthesis," often credited to the Anglo-American trio of Fisher, Haldane, and Wright. These included the concepts of the gene pool and genetic drift. He went to Columbia University and joined forces with Simpson, Ernst Mayr, and others who together brought the theory of evolution into respectability again. Ernst Mayr told the author that, when he came to Harvard in the early 1950s, there hadn't been a course in evolution taught there for over twenty-five years. He started the first modern evolution course at Harvard in 1952.

It is well known that Karl Marx, although born a Jew, had renounced all religion in favor of atheism but he had no real scientific basis for his faith until Darwin came along. He was so enamored with Darwin that he offered to dedicate his book *Das Kapital* to him.

For a time, some influential scientists in Russia, such as Kammerer, Pavlov, and Lysenko, began to favor Lamarckism over the uniformitarianism of Darwinism. But unlike the tautologies in Darwinism, Lamarckism could be tested. Finally, when it had been thoroughly falsified it was officially repudiated.

Regardless of the well-known objections, both social and

scientific, to the theory of punctuated equilibria evolution, it has within the last decade virtually swept aside all competition and become accepted by the vast majority of evolutionists in the United States. Stephen Jay Gould was chosen as "Man-of-the-Year in Science" by *Discover* magazine and appeared on the cover of *Newsweek*. The educational system is slow to be turned from a pervasive course, however, and few textbooks even mention punctuated equilibria theory a decade after it was first widely publicized.

Are Fossils Forming Today?

Since the late 1700s and early 1800s, the central unifying theme in geology and paleontology has been the idea that, with rare exception, all fossil-bearing geologic deposits were laid down slowly and gradually by uniform processes similar to those going on today. The slogan has been "the present is the key to the past." Because of this it was given the name "uniformitarianism." No significant catastrophes have been considered possible in this interpretive framework except local floods, volcanic eruptions and hurricanes. In fact, it was formulated for the explicit purpose of wiping out the centuries-old idea that there could have been a worldwide flood that once covered the entire earth with water. The uniformitarianists and catastrophists have been bitter rivals for the past 200 years. It can be stated quite properly that the uniformitarianists finally won the battle when evolution, its companion theory, became universally taught throughout public education institutions in the 1950s and 1960s. But not quite. There remained a few pockets of stubborn resistance — and not just among the creationists.

A noncreationist, Immanuel Velikovsky, was destined to put the first significant crack in the solid uniformitarianism edifice that had been built up in the natural science field. His first book, *Worlds in Collision,* published by Macmillan in 1950, postulated near misses of planets and comets in the fairly recent past.[18] Immediately, the book was enveloped in furious controversy, and Macmillan, intimidated by threats from academicians and scientists who wrote and bought textbooks, transferred the book to Doubleday. At the time, it was the number one best-seller in the nation.

Another book by Velikovsky, *Earth in Upheaval*, gave an even more convincing case for worldwide catastrophism.[19] While the earlier book included extensive documentation from literature and folklore showing that every civilization had witnessed cosmic disturbances, this book contained a massive amount of geological and paleontological evidence showing that catastrophes were the primary mechanism for fossil deposition and formation. It also gave evidence that conflicted with Darwinism.

At first the scientific community was solidly opposed to Velikovsky, and it gave him very shoddy treatment, calling him a heretic. But after over 50 of his predictions were shown to be correct through space program research, some scientists began to reconsider his ideas.

Although today few conventional astronomers agree with some of his hypotheses about the recent interaction among Mars, Venus and Earth, close encounters of Earth and comets or stars are now openly discussed. In fact, most of the recent geological conferences have been dominated by discussions of worldwide catastrophes which caused mass extinctions of almost all life — perhaps 96% of the species.

The 19 April 1984 issue of *Nature* magazine devoted over two pages to editorials and eleven pages to five articles on periodic mass extinctions. Editor John Maddox lectured his readers on why it was important to remain open-minded on the postulated causes of these catastrophes. He noted that the papers all referred to one given by David M. Raup and J. John Sepkoski, now both at the University of Chicago, and that they had "prevailed while others advocating periodic extinctions have done less well." He wrote, "But it is proper to acknowledge that the intellectual climate has changed in favour of catastrophism...."[20]

So, we have experienced a complete revolution in evolutionary-uniformitarian thinking over the past 30 years. It went from no worldwide catastrophes depositing fossils to one catastrophe about every 26 million years. This is no insignificant development in a field where there has been so much dogmatism and resistance to any consideration of possible error.

One not afraid to challenge the establishment, Stephen Gould, recognized the inevitable shift when he said:

> To many scientists, natural cataclysm seemed as threatening as the reign of terror...yet the geologic record seemed to provide as much evidence for cataclysmic as for gradual change....Contrary to popular myths, Darwin and Lyell were not the heroes of true science, defending objectivity against the teleological fantasies of such 'castastrophists' as Cuvier and Buckland. Catastrophists were as committed to science as any gradualist, in fact, they adopted the more 'objective' view that one should believe what one sees and not interpolate missing bits of gradual record into a literal tale of rapid change.[21]

What is some of the evidence for catastrophism which has impressed Gould and others? One of the main pieces of evidence is the presence of massive fossil graveyards around the world. It is only reasonable to ask whether any of these could have been laid down by currently operating processes. Is there any evidence of significant fossil formation presently taking place?

All of the museum officials interviewed were asked if there was any example they could identify of significant fossil deposition going on today on the bottom of any lake, sea or ocean. Their replies were unanimous. Dr. Patterson said, "The only cases I know about are some dead fish that were dredged up from the bottom of the Black Sea and off the coast of South Africa 500 feet below the surface of the water. There is no way of knowing why they are lying on the bottom or if there are significant numbers of them. Perhaps they floated to the surface and burst. They are not fossils yet." Could they be compared to the billions of fish thrown together, all contorted in the Lompoc formation of California? "No, not like the Lompoc. These things are scattered and they are rare."

Dr. Fisher was asked if he knew of any examples today where fish were being fossilized on the bottom of any sea floor.

He replied, "I can't give you any specific examples, but I'm sure that they are finding them on the sea floor today. . . . When the skeletons fall to the sea floor, I'm sure that a certain percentage of those are being covered with sediment." Did he have any firsthand knowledge? His reply was in the negative: "Did I see it? I haven't seen it, no." Neither had he heard of any. He was told: "See, this is where we are trying to sift out, the conjecture from the facts. The conjecture is that these thick layers of fish fossils were formed over millions of years as sediments covered the dead fish, but we don't find them on the bottom of any ocean, sea, or lake. . . . Normally a dead fish just floats to the surface and is consumed." Dr. Fisher thought that the reason we did not see evidence of fish forming into fossils was that "man has such a short span of life that he can't observe these things happening." The only example he could give of anything fossilizing in New York State was leaves that had fallen into mineral water becoming coated with minerals.

The author continued questioning Dr. Fisher about the lack of organisms in the process of fossilization: "Still we have billions and billions of fossils all thrown together. For instance, down at Glen Rose, Texas, Dr. Steve Austin, a geologist, told me that he found something just as significant as the many dinosaur and human tracks there. This was a three-foot layer of pelecypods (clams) all with their valves (shells) closed. How could pelecypods get formed into fossils over millions of years without their valves opening? They had to have been covered suddenly."

Dr. Fisher agreed, "Oh yes. We've seen that with brachiopods here in New York. We have brachiopods with their valves closed. There had to have been a catastrophic covering of sediments." He thought there were many catastrophes that formed the fossils, but he did not think they were on a worldwide scale. That was before there was so much talk about catastrophism at the geology conferences.

Hardy-Weinberg Principle

High school biology students in New York State, and perhaps across the country, must struggle with what is called the Hardy-Weinberg principle. This involves the use of a complex equation, called a quadratic, that is supposed to describe how populations of organisms change. It is a most difficult thing for students who have not had algebra to cope with but it has the effect of making evolution theory appear to be well-defined mathematically. Students are thus inclined to believe it despite the fact that they have not the slightest idea of what Hardy-Weinberg means. The principle is stated thus:

> If mating is random (naturally breeding) in a given large population and no external factors are involved, the gene frequencies (percentage of occurrence of particular genes) and the genetic proportions in the population will remain constant from generation to generation. By definition this is a stable population.

This is a statistical rule that can only come into play when the population is large, is naturally interbreeding, has no mutations, and has no migrating elements. If mating is not random but directed in some way by external factors, the population is not stable and changes genetically. These changes often alter the outward appearance of the population. The big question is whether the change is ever in a direction that would produce basically new genetic material so that a previously nonexistent structure or function comes into being.

Case after case can be cited where populations have been irradiated and deliberately mutated, but they have never been observed to change into anything basically different from the original — a bacterium is always a bacterium, a fruit fly is always a fruit fly, a dog is always a dog.

Evolutionists classify some of this observable variation as speciation, however, someone calling a variation by a new species name does not prove that all life evolved from a common ancestor. Even when a phenomenon called polyploidy occurs and the number of chromosomes is doubled in an offspring, the plant (or occasionally animal) never changes into anything other than a variant of the original. A flower is still the same kind of flower, a salamander is still a salamander, etc.

Here is how Dr. Eldredge explained it: Initially things are in equilibrium, and then certain conditions are needed to disrupt the equilibrium. Then a new state of equilibrium is reached. He said, "In my mind, Hardy-Weinberg and all of the other formulas on population genetics show how difficult a job it is to change a characteristic." That, indeed, is a true assessment. That is why Dr. Eldredge observed that stasis was one of the two most significant characteristics of the fossil record. When he observed the second important fact, which is the sudden appearance of new species, it is simply an assumption that the new species, with totally different structures, had evolved from some other ones.

Dr. Patterson commented on the statement that the Hardy-Weinberg principle showed stability: "Yes. It has nothing to do with evolution. People keep asking me why I didn't mention it in my book. Ha! Ha! It has nothing to do with evolution. Everytime I find a population it's inside Hardy-Weinberg equilibrium."

Population Genetics

One of the ideas that the revised Darwinism was supposed to have contributed to biology was the contention that individuals do not evolve, populations evolve: populations would become isolated and drift, gradually forming a new species. Norman Macbeth had some comments about the contribution of so-called population genetics to science:

> Lewontin says some shocking things too, but some of these men are regarded as "enfants terribles" who like to startle people. The profession as a whole settles right back into its normal routine and ignores them.

> I wrote a paper recently on the subject of population genetics with a neighbor who is a professor of zoology. We discovered that the three leading recent treatises on population genetics, one by Lewontin, one by Spiess and another by Jonathan Roughgarden at Stanford, all stated that population genetics had contributed nothing to evolution theory. Therefore, our paper said that we didn't

see any reason why courses in evolution should waste any time on population genetics.

One of our colleagues at a nearby college read it over and said, "I really agree with you; this is all true, but you can't publish that. Publish that and the creationists will get hold of it and throw it in our faces." There is still a conscious effort to cover up problems with evolution. This professor didn't quite realize what she was saying, and if we had pointed out that this was just sweeping it under the rug, she might have changed her position. But they instinctively take this position and try to protect the traditional and sacred theories that were taught to them in school and that they've been teaching to their own students. You have to wonder where they would be if they did say this had all been a lot of rubbish.

We had in that article that Gene Fairley called both Gregory Bateson and Marshall Sahlins and asked them what they thought of his creation myth theory — that Darwinism was a creation myth and you don't question creation myths. These two anthropologists answered, "That's not a bad idea." Bateson said, "I've just written something on that myself" and he read off a very sarcastic note about natural selection. "Wonderful theory," he said, "it demonstrates that if things are the way they are, they tend to remain the way they are. It's about as stupid as that."

Sahlins in Chicago said, "That's not a bad idea. I never thought of it before, but it is all right. But why are you so excited about natural selection anyway? Natural selection is all bunk. . . . On the tape he said, "Science is like an eclair, it's firm on the outside but it is all mushy on the inside. It is good in the eating, however, so we enjoy it and go on with it." These are terrible confessions.[22]

It was noted that those are the confessions of honest scientists and Macbeth replied, "They are outside the gang that have staked their life on it (evolution)."

Embryology

Although Darwin recognized that the fossil record did not give any support for the theory of evolution, he was most impressed by what he thought was the best evidence for common ancestry of all life, namely, embryological development. He said that it was "second to none in importance." The hypothesis that during embryological development higher organisms, like man, relived their evolutionary history was popularized by Ernst Haeckel in Germany at about the time Darwinism was gaining acceptance. The concept, however, was originated in 1811 by Johann Meckel before scientists took the theory of evolution seriously. He thought that the embryonic stages of development in higher forms of life paralleled the adult stages of lower forms. Fifteen years later Karl von Baer argued that it was the embryonic stages of lower forms rather than the adult stages which were paralleled by higher forms. Then, in 1864, Fritz Muller proposed that the higher forms added stages to the embryonic stages passed through by the lower forms in their development. Ernst Haeckel, in 1866, simply combined the ideas of others and popularized the theory which he called "the fundamental biogenetic law."

Haeckel, demonstrating his considerable artistic skills, made wood carvings which indicated that the embryos of a fish, tortoise, hare, pig, monkey, and man had similar appearances at various stages. He was one of Charles Darwin's staunchest supporters and claimed that his discoveries validated the theory that all life had come from a common ancestor.

Since a law in science is generally recognized as a hypothesis or theory that has withstood many years of testing without experiencing a single disproof, Haeckel's calling this idea a "law" was stretching the term by no small amount. After over 150 years of testing in the laboratory, the biogenetic law has not fared very well. Let us examine the record to see if it deserves to be called a law.

The natural history museum experts interviewed by the author were not specialists in the field of embryology so the subject was only discussed with two, Drs. Raup and Patterson. Dr. Raup was well aware of the current feeling in scientific

circles about the theory. He said, "The biogenetic law —
embryologic recapitulation — I think, was debunked back in
the 1920s by embryologists. I don't see embryology as any
different than any other kind of comparative morphology,
similarities being in (embryonic) stages or in adult morphology."

Famous anthropologist professor Ashley Montagu, in a
debate with Dr. Duane Gish on 12 April 1980 at Princeton
University, verified Dr. Raup's claim that the "law" had been
debunked in the 1920s. First Dr. Gish commented on the
harmful effects of evolution theory on research:

> Years and years of embryological research was
> essentially wasted because people, convinced of the
> theory of evolution and that embryos recapitulated
> their evolutionary ancestry, spent much of their
> time in embryological research trying to develop
> phylogenies based on the data of embryology. As
> I mentioned earlier, embryologists have abandoned
> the theory of embryological recapitulation. They
> don't believe it. They know it is not true. . . . It pro-
> duced bad research rather than the good research
> that should have been done.

In response, Dr. Montagu stated:

> The theory of recapitulation was destroyed in
> 1921 by Professor Walter Garstang in a famous
> paper, since when no respectable biologist has ever
> used the theory of recapitulation, because it was
> utterly unsound, created by a Nazi-like preacher
> named Haeckel.

Dr. Gish made a further comment:

> Ladies and gentlemen, I have traveled all over the
> world. I have debated and lectured on many, many
> major university campuses, and it is hardly a single
> university campus that I appear on that some stu-
> dent does not tell me that he is taught the theory of
> embryological recapitulation right there at that
> university. I've had many evolutionists argue the
> evidence for evolution from embryological recapitu-
> lation. Unfortunately, as Dr. Montagu has said,

it is a thoroughly discredited theory, but it is still taught in most biology books and in most universities and schools as evidence for evolution.

Dr. Montagu then made a most perceptive observation:
Well ladies and gentlemen, that only goes to show that many so-called educational institutions, called universities, are not educational institutions at all or universities; they are institutes for miseducation.[23]

At the time of the interview, Dr. Patterson must not have been aware that recapitulation theory had fallen into disrepute for he said that he felt comfortable with it and that it was still alive: "It's one of the few things that I think has survived. The expectation in Darwin's time was that all we need do was look at fossils and they would give us the answers. But it's true to say they haven't. I do like the ideas of embryology. That's one of the few things that has stood the test of time." When asked if he was aware that the human embryo at no time was anthropoid in appearance but that the ape embryo appears humanoid at one point and so was backwards, he replied, "It's only backwards if you insist that man is the highest point in the evolutionary tree, which I wouldn't try to say." Since the interview, Dr. Patterson has become an antievolutionist so perhaps he has changed his beliefs about the evidence from embryology.

It is significant that the *Encyclopedia Britannica* in its extensive discussion of embryological development, under the section on zoology, contains only two sentences about Haeckel and his biogenetic law. In its biographical sketch of him it states, "Haeckel was the originator of the dictum that, 'ontogeny recapitulates phylogeny,' since proved to be false.[24] Strangely, it did not mention the well-known fact that Haeckel forged some of his drawings of embryos to make them appear in accord with his theory, and used the same sketches to represent several different animals. He was even accused of altering drawings of embryos made by others. For his forgery, he was convicted by a German court. His forgeries were brought to the attention of the public in 1911 in a book called *Haeckel's Frauds and Forgeries*.[25] In view of the fact that the problems were well known from the very beginning, it is inexplicable that this theory of recapitulation ever gained such widespread acceptance before being debunked in the nineteen-hundreds. Professor Kerkut of the University of Southampton quotes Radl as saying, "Everything that has ever been cited against the theory was known when the theory was put forward; nevertheless it was widely accepted. Today some still accept it, others do not."[26]

In his *A History of Biology*, Charles Singer discussed Haeckel's influence on science: "His faults are not hard to see. For a generation and more he purveyed to the semi-educated public a system of the crudest philosophy — if a mass of contradictions can be called by that name. He founded something that wore the habiliments of a religion, of which he was at once the high priest and the congregation."[27]

Why do modern embryologists not believe in embryological recapitulation? First, when scientists studied the embryological development of various animals and got beyond the superficial appearance level, they soon discovered that no higher embryo develops along the same route as is assumed for common-ancestry evolution. There are just too many exceptions for the theory to have any credence. In fact, many structures develop in an order that is the reverse of that assumed for evolution.

The most popular evidence offered to support recapitulation is the presence of so-called "gill slits" in the embryos of fish, mammals, and human beings at a certain stage of development. This is supposed to show that man and other mammals came from an ancestral fish. It is true that the embryos of these animals have a series of folds in the tissue of the neck region. In the fish embryo the gills develop in this region, but in mammals they never form slits and are never part of the respiratory system. These folds transform into other organs having no connection with respiration, which in mammals is accomplished through the placenta. If they are never slits and are never gills, they could hardly be honestly called "gill slits."

Some of the numerous facts of embryonic development that contradict recapitulation theory are: Evolution was supposed to have created teeth before the tongue, but children develop the tongue before teeth. Vertebrate embryos form the heart before the remainder of the circulatory system, but evolution theory holds that the opposite occurred. The human embryo never has a tail with extra vertebrae extending far beyond the pelvis. Rather, the pelvis forms near the tip of the spinal column, which quite naturally develops first.

The October 1979 issue of *Parents' Magazine* contains some impressive color photographs of the developing human embryo photographed with a technique involving fiber optics. The article notes that "Since the human embryo has been photographed at every stage of development, it is now known to be specifically human at every stage."[28]

Even though knowledgeable embryologists have abandoned the discredited theory of embryological recapitulation, it is likely to retain its place in school and university textbooks for many years. In April 1984 it was still being taught in Ivy League colleges where the author lectured. Yesterday's myths die hard, especially when they so nicely help to perpetuate a particular favored philosophical belief system.

Homology

Another bit of indirect evidence that evolutionists since the time of Erasmus Darwin have used to argue in support of their theory is the similarity in certain structures in otherwise basically different groups of organisms. For example, the bones in the forelimbs of man, horse, bat, whale and dog share certain superficial structural similarities. The homologous structures are supposed to indicate that their possessors all came from a common ancestor. This is one of the most logically appealing arguments used by evolution theory protagonists because it appears to be supported by visually observable evidence that can be readily perceived.

Certainly, similarities in organisms can indicate closeness of relationship, but this is not a dependable guide because there are many cases of close similarity that could not be due to inheritance from a recent common ancestor. If similarities show evolutionary relationship, then dissimilarities should conversely show a lack of relationship. The rule should be consistently applied not simply ignored when the evidence conflicts with it.

The following structures are very similar to those in humans: The octopus eye, pig heart, Pekingese dog's face, milk of the ass and the pronator quadratus muscle of the Japanese salamander. When the concentration of red blood cells is considered, man is more similar to frogs, fish, and birds than to sheep. Do these homologies indicate close evolutionary relationships? Obviously not. There could hardly be two organisms further apart on the assumed evolutionary tree than the octopus and man, and two placental mammals are much closer on the evolutionary tree than man and fish or man and bird.

There are many more dissimilarities in the organisms that possess homologous structures, but evolutionists ignore them when looking for evidence to support their theory. For example, in the three thousand different species of frogs in which there are many superficial similarities, there is much greater variation in their DNA than there is between the bat and the blue whale, which structurally are vastly different.

It is absolutely unacceptable in the field of science for a researcher to carefully select his data and cover up that which contradicts his theory. But that is done repeatedly in this particular branch of science. It is permitted because of the widespread philosophical bias among scientists, which causes them not to publicize evidence that discredits evolution.

Frequently, apologists for recognized abuses in evolutionary science use the excuse that there are other branches of science such as molecular physics which also cannot have all of their theories tested empirically. This might be true, but one fault is never justified by the revelation of another one of equal magnitude.

The above discussion, however, is admittedly somewhat subjective. It is not necessary to consider only such superficialities now that the science of genetics has progressed to the point where we can observe the genes that control specific structures. In his 1974 book, *Homology an Unsolved Problem,* prominent British evolutionist Gavin de Beer stated:

It is now clear that the pride with which it was

assumed that the inheritance of homologous structures from a common ancestor explained homology
was misplaced; for such inheritance cannot be
ascribed to identity of genes. The attempt to find
homologous genes has been given up as hopeless...
what mechanism can it be that results in the production of homologous organs, the same patterns, in
spite of their NOT being controlled by the same
genes: I asked this question in 1938, and it has not
been answered. It is useless to speculate on any
explanation in the absence of facts.[29]

Since evolution is supposed to be a change in the genes
which changes the structures that they control, how could the
structures remain virtually unchanged but the genes that
control them become changed completely? William Fix
quoted Randall, who described the situation very clearly:

The older text-books on evolution make much of
the idea of homology, pointing out the obvious
resemblances between the skeletons of the limbs of
different animals. Thus the "pentadactyl" limb
pattern is found in the arm of a man, the wing of a
bird, and the flipper of a whale, and this is held to
indicate their common origin. Now if these various
structures were transmitted by the same gene-
complex, varied from time to time by mutations and
acted upon by environmental selection, the theory
would make good sense. Unfortunately this is not
the case. Homologous organs are now known to be
produced by totally different gene complexes in
the different species. The concept of homology in
terms of similar genes handed on from a common
ancestor has broken down....[30]

How one views the similarities and differences in different
organisms depends entirely on the philosophical bias of the
individual. But good science should be practiced in a manner
that is independent, as much as humanly possible, from
individual biases of investigators. The safest conclusion one
might draw from the evidence of homologies is that it doesn't
necessarily indicate whether organisms evolved from a com-

mon ancestor or were created by an intelligent designer. It can be stated with complete confidence that the resolution of that question is beyond the bounds of empirical science.

Different Names for Same Species

An unusual practice among paleontologists was uncovered during the interviews, namely, that of giving different names to the same species if it is found in rocks of different periods. Dr. Eldredge was asked, "Do paleontologists name the same creatures differently when they are found in different geological periods?" He replied that this happens, but they are mistakes. When asked the same question, Dr. Patterson replied, "Oh yes, that's very widely done." Next he was asked, "That doesn't seem quite honest. You wouldn't do that, would you?" He said that he hoped he wouldn't. Dr. Raup was asked, "In these books it is claimed that paleontologists call the same creature by different species names when it is found in different period rocks. Is that true?" He acknowledged that it used to be a very common practice and still occurred. How did this happen? If a fossil were found in South America that was indistinguishable from one previously found in Europe, many taxonomists would give it a different name. He said that this was partly due to some evolutionary model that they were using which made them think that a species could not have lasted such a long time or covered such a wide geographic area. It was done purposely because of an *a priori* theoretical model, but he thought that most of these had "been cleaned out now."

Would not this practice make a lot more species? Dr. Raup said that it would; perhaps 70 percent of the species described are later found to be the same as existing species, so 70 percent of the new species named should not have been, either through ignorance or because of the ground rules used by the taxonomists.

How do taxonomists establish a new species? Dr. Raup said that if you can not find a description of the organism, and, in your judgment, it is sufficiently different from any other to have been reproductively isolated, then it is given a new species name. An assistant of Dr. Eldredge who was studying trilobite fossils as the American Museum explained to the author how he made the decision on naming a new species: "I look at a fossil for about two weeks and then if I think it is different enough, I give it a new name." So it is simply a matter of judgment with no firm ground rules. Obviously it is impossible to check the reproductive isolation of a fossil.

Chapter 6

Darwinism's Lack of Scientific Foundation

Can Randomness Produce Ordered Systems?

The fossil record makes it eminently clear that the history of life on Earth did not include a progressive development from a common ancestor. At least, if it did so, it left absolutely no sign of the process in the rock record. But, regardless of the lack of fossil evidence for common-ancestry evolution, many people have faith that, given enough time, random processes could produce almost any degree of complexity. The idea of randomness as opposed to some deterministic force was a primary contention of Charles Darwin.

As Stephen Jay Gould wrote in an introduction to *What Darwin Really Said*, "Darwin also introduced the specter of randomness into evolutionary theory. To be sure, randomness only provides a source of *variation* in Darwin's theory. Natural selection (a deterministic process) then scrutinizes the spectrum of random variants and preserves those individuals best adapted to changing local environments."[1] In other words, the raw material on which natural selection operates is generated exclusively by random variations. The only qualifier added is that there is a finite number of possible combinations inherent in the genetic code. The total number of possible messages in DNA is so enormous, however, that it imposes no practical restriction on the evolutionary process.

On 22 April 1984, Dr. Gould had not changed his opinion that evolution was purely an accidental process, for on the television program *60 Minutes* he said:

> If the history of life teaches us any lesson, it is
> that human beings arose as a kind of glorious
> accident...surely a kind of glorious cosmic
> accident resulting from the catenation (linking) of
> thousands of improbable events."

He very accurately described the core of evolutionary faith
— that man is the product of an immense number of glorious
accidents which linked together a continuous series of improbable events. Let us see what modern science has to say
about such grandiose terms as "glorious cosmic accident" and
"catenation of thousands of improbable events."

Have we learned anything in the past century that would
indicate how a purely random process could generate the
raw material that would allow another naturalistic process,
natural selection, to weed out the less fit and preserve only the
better fitted? For the answer it is necessary to turn to other
scientific disciplines such as mathematics.

In 1966, after the advent of the tremendously powerful
analytical tool, the digital computer, biologist Dr. Martin
Kaplan organized a symposium at the Wistar Institute in
Philadelphia to thoroughly air a dispute between leading
mathematicians and evolutionary biologists. The dispute
had come to light at several meetings the previous year in
Switzerland between mathematicians and biologists who were
discussing mathematical doubts concerning the Darwinian
theory of evolution. At the end of several hours of heated
debate, the biologists proposed that a symposium be arranged
to consider the points of dispute more systematically and
with a more powerful array of biologists who could function
adequately in the realm of mathematics. The Wistar symposium was the result.[2]

In his preface to the proceedings of the symposium, Dr.
Kaplan commented about the importance of mathematics
in such matters as theorizing about origins. He said that to
construct a history of thought without profound study of the
mathematical ideas of successive efforts is comparable to
omitting the part of Ophelia from Shakespeare's play,
Hamlet.

The fifty-two attendees included a dazzling array of evolutionary biologists such as Sidney Fox, Ernst Mayr, George Wald, Richard Lewontin, Loren Eiseley and H.B.D. Kettlewell of peppered moth fame from England. The mathematicians included Murray Eden and V.F. Weisskopf of MIT, Marcel Schutzenberger of Paris, and Stanislaw Ulam of Los Alamos. This was a conference to end all such conferences — and it apparently did as nothing like it has been held since.

Nobel Prize laureate and biologist Peter Medawar chaired the symposium. He stated its purpose in his opening remarks: "As Dr. Kaplan has explained, the immediate cause of this conference is a pretty widespread sense of dissatisfaction about what has come to be thought of as the accepted evolutionary theory in the English-speaking world, the so-called neo-Darwinian Theory. This dissatisfaction has been expressed from three quarters and is not only scientific." He listed the three main objections to neo-Darwinian theory as first, religious; second, philosophical and methodological; and finally, "Objections by fellow scientists who feel that, in the current theory, something is missing." He said, "These objections to current neo-Darwinian theory are very widely held among biologists generally; and we must on no account, I think, make light of them."[3]

Loren Eiseley also indicated a need for the symposium in view of the fact that there were still some unanswered questions about a mechanism for evolution. He noted that Darwin had placed emphasis on "fortuitous variation and selection" in the evolutionary process. He thought that Darwin's use of "fortuitous" in terms of pure chance and "mysterious laws" could be made allowance for because of what he did not know about genetics. But he said, "I still think Darwin expressed a certain tolerance, a marked degree of wary unease, as to whether, indeed, the phrase "fortuitous variation" was a sufficient answer to all our problems."[4] This was the primary problem addressed by the symposium: Is there some natural process, which can be defined mathematically, that could generate the raw material which the theory of evolution requires as the first step in the creation of every different type of living organism?

For two days the biologists and mathematicians examined the question from every possible angle. Murray Eden, in a paper entitled, "Inadequacies of Neo-Darwinian Evolution as a Scientific Theory," showed that it would be unlikely for even a single ordered pair of genes to be produced by mutations in the DNA of the bacteria, *E. coli*, in five billion years. He calculated that, to have any reasonable chance of getting such a result, you would need a population of that organism weighing a hundred trillion tons, enough to cover the entire Earth to a thickness of nearly an inch. He contended that the only way to overthrow this calculation was "by finding of a new *determinate* feature," in other words, a new natural law.[5] This relates to only the probability of getting just one ordered pair of genes, but hundreds of genes are present in this bacterium. In fact, it is estimated that the genes of *E. coli* contain over a trillion (10^{12}) bits of data. That is the number ten followed by twelve zeros. Dr. Eden also calculated the maximum number of protein molecules that could have existed on Earth in ten billion years, and it is only an "infinitesimal number" when compared to the maximum number of possibilities in a polypeptide chain containing 250 links.

These calculations are consistent with those made earlier by the French scientist, Lecomte du Nouy, who examined the mathematical odds of life having evolved by chance from nonliving matter. Regarding the formation of a single protein, he said that the "time needed to form, on an average, one such molecule in a material volume equal to that of our terrestrial globe is about 10^{243} years."[6] Thus, he concluded that the odds against the chance formation of a single protein were so great that such an event could not have occurred.

Dr. Eden attacked the central tenet of evolution, natural selection. He said, "Concepts such as natural selection by the survival of the fittest are tautologous; that is, they simply restate the fact that only the properties of organisms which survive to produce offspring, or to produce more offspring than their cohorts, will appear in succeeding generations." He further explained, "Any principal criticism of current thoughts on evolutionary theory is directed to the strong use of the notion of 'randomness' in selection. The process of speciation by a mechanism of random variation of properties in offspring is usually too imprecisely defined to be tested. When it is precisely defined, it is highly implausible."[7]

Getting away from the philosophical discussion, Dr. Eden reported on his extensive genetic data on hemoglobin. Hemoglobin contains two chains, called alpha and beta. Evolutionists assume that one evolved from the other through certain random mutations. He said that it would take a minimum of 120 point mutations to convert alpha to beta. At least 34 of these mutations required changing two or three nucleotides of the 140 residues in the chain. Yet, if a single nucleotide change occurs through mutation the result is highly deleterious to the organism.

George Wald commented on just this point. He said that George Gaylord Simpson of Harvard had claimed that all changes in protein were adaptive. Because of this remark, Dr. Wald said he "took a little trouble to find whether a single amino acid change in a hemoglobin mutation is known that doesn't affect seriously the function of that hemoglobin. One is hard put to find such an instance. Do you understand what I am saying?....One is hard put to find a single instance in which a change in one amino acid in sequence does not change markedly the properties."[8] For example, the change of one amino acid out of 287 in hemoglobin causes sickle-cell anemia. Molecules of normal hemoglobin have a glutamic acid unit where the sickle-cell hemoglobin has a valine unit. The resulting disease kills about 25 percent of the population of black humans who are affected. (Evolutionists often like to cite this highly deleterious mutation as a good example of a beneficial mutation because those afflicted with sickle-cell anemia are less likely to die with malaria. To the overall population, however, it is highly destructive.) Dr. Wald also noted the enormous time span required to establish a mutation in a population: "If you make a rough estimate..., it looks as if something of the order of ten million years is needed to establish a mutation. That is, each of these single amino acid changes appears relatively frequently in individuals as pathology; but to establish one such change as a regular characteristic in a species seems to take something of the order of ten million years."[9]

Participants in the symposium said that obviously there must be a way for nature to reduce the odds against evolution, but no one could offer a mathematical characterization of such a mechanism. Dr. Eden said, "What I would like to find is the characterization of these constraints. . . . What I am claiming is simply that without some constraint on the notion of random variation, in either the properties of the organism or the sequence of the DNA, there is no particular reason to expect that we could have gotten any kind of viable form other than nonsense."[10] He was talking explicitly about the very heart of the question of plausibility in macroevolution. If the raw material of evolutionary change is supposed to be generated by random processes, and random processes cannot be shown to produce even a fraction of the intelligence contained in the simplest DNA, then some nonrandom mechanism must be found. When no such mechanism can be found, the theory should be deposited in the rubbish heap. Natural selection is sometimes offered by neophytes as the answer, but knowledgeable specialists in the field know that selection cannot operate until there is raw material for it to preserve.

The problem becomes even more insurmountable when considering the matter of prebiology, or the origin of the first living cell from nonliving chemicals. Some participants preferred not to address that subject, claiming that it was not a part of evolution, but Sidney Fox disagreed. Dr. Fox made the inexplicable statement that the evolutionary process from non-life to life was one of decreasing order and was completely in accord with the second law of thermodynamics that edicts this running down in all closed systems. He said, "On the premise of a logical evolutionary span from prelife to life and from pre-protein to protein, the total picture is one of an evolution from a highly ordered primordial state to a considerably less ordered state, when looked at purely from the standpoint of the protein. This progression is in keeping with the second law of thermodynamics. . . ."[11] This statement is particularly astounding since the simplest living cell contains over a trillion bits of data in its genes — a number equivalent to the total number of letters in all the books in the world's largest library. If the supposed natural process from nonlife to life represents a loss of intelligence, Dr. Fox is asking a lot if he expects anyone to believe that chemicals in an ancient ocean could contain more data than is in the largest library. It is quite understandable that most attendees were happy to avoid a discussion of the origin of life.

Ernst Mayr made some startling admissions about Darwin's original model of mutation and natural selection. He said, "Popper is right; this model is so good that it can explain everything, as Popper has rightly complained."[12] This relates to the requirement in science that a theory or model must make exclusionary predictions. If the concept is so generalized that it can explain any conceivable type of evidence, then it is of no value in science. For example, if a theory can explain both dark and light coloration in moths, both the presence and absence of transitional forms in the fossil record, complex life forms either above or below in rock strata, etc., then it has no value in making predictions. Dr. Mayr talked in generalities about neo-Darwinism being more than just mutation and natural selection — gene flow from one population to another, for example. But he admitted that, in reality, the raw material was all generated by random mutations: "Ultimately, all variation is, of course, due to mutation....The input of untested new mutations in these cases would almost invariably have a deleterious effect."[13] At the conclusion of his comments he could only offer this in regard to a mathematical definition of his neo-Darwinism model that could be tested on a computer: "I think it should mean one thing in particular, which is that the approach adopted should not be too simplistic."[14] From this, one can only gather that he admits that there is no presently known, definitive theory on how life could have evolved from a common ancestor by a materialistic process. The challenge to define the theory mathematically quickly strips its proponents of the endless verbiage containing generalizations and suppositions. He added during the ensuing discussion, "Whenever a major new evolutionary branch originates, whether the birds, or the first mammals, or any other major new taxon, *it always goes in an incredibly short time* (geologically speaking) through that labile stage between the well-defined ancestral phenotype and the new descendant type. This is what was such a puzzle to Goldschmidt.... An Eocene bat looks just like a modern bat."[15] In this manner, Dr. Mayr copes with the total lack of fossilized transitional forms between the major different kinds of life.

In a discussion of how evolution theory can explain the fact that eels which normally reproduce only in salt water have certain landlocked species that reproduce in fresh water, Dr. Weisskopt said, "I think it was Medawar who said that one thing about the theory of evolution is (and he quoted Popper) that it is not falsifiable, that whatever happens you can always explain it. I think you have an example here."[16]

On the same subject, Dr. Fraser said, "It would seem to me that there have been endless statements made and the only thing I have clearly agreed with through the whole day has been the statement made by Karl Popper, namely, that the real inadequacy of evolution, esthetically and scientifically, is that you can explain anything you want by changing your variables around."[17]

George Wald agreed: "This cannot be done in evolution, taking it in its broad sense, and this is really all I meant when I called it tautologous in the first place. It can, indeed, explain anything. You may be ingenious or not in proposing a mechanism which looks plausible to human beings... but it is still an unfalsifiable theory."[18]

Dr. Schutzenberger of the University of Paris reported on why all attempts to program a model of evolution on a computer had completely failed. He said that neo-Darwinism asserts that without anything further, selection brings about a statistically adapted drift when random changes are performed in a population. He insisted, "We believe that it is not conceivable. In fact if we try to simulate such a situation by making changes randomly at the typographic level (by letters or blocks, the size of the unit does not really matter). On computer programs we find that we have no chance (i.e. less than one in ten to the thousandth power) even to see what the modified program would compute: it just jams." In conclusion, Dr. Schutzenberger said, "Thus... we believe that there is a considerable gap in the neo-Darwinian theory of evolution, and we believe this gap to be of such a nature that it cannot be bridged within the current conception of biology."[19]

One problem of course is that regardless of all the discoveries we have made in the field of genetics, there still is no way to know how chains of nucleic acids in DNA instruct the cell to perform its multitudinous and complex functions. Dr. Ulam said, "Nobody in the nineteenth century or even now would profess to understand the details of how, from the code, an actual organism is produced."[20] To this Schutzenberger replied that, if there were explicit general principles relating them we should be able to simulate them and show the passage from disorder to order. He insisted that with even the simple models that had been programmed on the computer, "What we know is that when we make changes of a typographic nature, most of them are meaningless from any respect, and when I say 'most of the them,' I mean less than one out of ten to the hundredth power."[21] In reply to Lewontin's claim that a very large proportion of mutations do not render the molecule meaningless, Schutzenberger said, "I ask you, what is the mechanism which makes it so, or what sort of conceptual mechanism could make it so? I don't know of any general principle or of any trick which in any other circumstances could produce this effect."[22] When someone argued in general terms about how evolution solved the problem, he replied that they were falling into a trap: "You only make the case worse by supposing that the mechanism which induces an agreement between the topologies has been produced also by random changes. That is to say, this sort of fallacy has been used a lot of times in 'artificial intelligence' to pretend that one could write programs [for] machines which would learn how to tell themselves how to improve programs."[23]

Dr. Waddington commented, "Your argument is simply that life must have come about by special creation."[24] This brought a resounding "No!"

Near the end of the symposium, Murray Eden presented a second paper that summarized the results of the encounter quite well. He said that, during the course of development of neo-Darwinian evolution, a variety of postulates have been suggested and invalidated, so:

"In consequence, the theory has been modified to

the point that virtually every formulation of the principles of evolution is a tautology....It is our contention that if 'random' is given a serious and crucial interpretation from a probabilistic point of view, the randomness postulate is highly implausible and that an adequate scientific theory of evolution must await the discovery and elucidation of new natural laws — physical, physico-chemical and biological....In summary, it is our contention that the principal task of the evolutionist is to discover and examine mechanisms which constrain the variation of phenotypes to a very small class and to relegate the notion of randomness to a minor non-crucial role."[25]

Darwin's main undertaking was to attempt to show how the great complexity found in the biosphere could be explained by some purely natural process free of any outside guiding force or intelligence. The mathematicians at this conference showed that the commonly assumed random process of mutation could not possibly produce the raw material for evolution even in many times the assumed age of the universe. So evolutionists are left with the task of discovering new natural laws if they are to justify not relegating their theory to the rubbish heap or restricting it to books on religion and philosophy.

What did the museum officials say in their interviews about mutations? Dr. Patterson said that whether there was such a thing as a beneficial mutation depended upon how you looked at it. He mentioned sickle-cell anemia and the generating of penicillin from mold as two candidates. Under certain circumstances, these could be considered good mutations. It was pointed out to him that in the delivery rooms of hospitals, evolutionists never hope for a mutation; yet, they say we got here by gradual mutations. He answered, "Right." It was also pointed out that, to the overall population, sickle-cell anemia was deleterious, and he replied, "Well, that is all anyone can say. Nobody would every say that all these mutations would be advantageous."

Question: "Dobzhansky, after years of irradiating fruit flies for thousands of generations to artificially induce mutations, couldn't think of a single mutant that was more viable out in nature. He could only think of several which might be more viable at unusual conditions like very elevated temperatures.'' To this Dr. Patterson agreed, and pointed out that his fruit flies were all in glass jars. What did he think of the mechanism for evolution? He said that he had to agree that the only known kind of mutation was spontaneous change.

Question: "It is claimed that organisms evolve or develop resistance to antibiotic drugs, but some bacteria frozen in 1946 before antibiotics were developed were found to be immune to as many as six different antibiotic drugs. So the resistance was already in a small proportion of the population, right?" Dr. Patterson agreed. The literature now says that resistance in some organisms is due to an extra-chromosomal material called plasmids which are passed on by conjugal union.

Dr. Eldredge was asked for an explanation of a mechanism for evolution. Did he agree with the view that it was natural selection working on random mutations? He said that this was the core of neo-Darwinism: more organisms are produced than can survive, a nonrandom pattern of survival. That was not what he believed but his rendition of the core of it. He said that mutations are random only in that they are not directed to help the individual. There is a limit to the kinds of mutations possible. Then natural selection selects out the most harmonious gene combinations. Did he think there were any beneficial mutations? He said, "Well that's not the point. The point is that amongst all the gene complexes that are produced in one generation (I'm just giving you my understanding) you are going to get some that are more harmonious than others. Maybe you are, maybe you aren't. We all know of people who have less chance of surviving and reproducing."

Dr. Eldredge then admitted, when questioned about sickle-cell anemia, that most mutations are harmful: "Apparently most mutations are harmful — that's an old story — because they foul up in the developmental process. They are mistakes in copying, that's what they are." He thought that he was compelled to accept, as a general proposition, that some of these mistakes in copying must have been improvements because things have changed.

Question: "(You mean) if evolution is true, that is?" Dr. Eldredge replied:

> Yes. Well I told you I have adopted a set of axioms. The single axiom is that I see two ways of explaining the nested sets of patterns and resemblances in the world. I have adopted as an axiom, just to see how far I could go with it, the evolution one because I think you can make more predictions and more statements. That's all I've said. It's not a matter of true belief.... The mistake that we have today I think is that the most powerful individuals — in the sense of the dynamism of their personalities, etc. — in the last generation more or less have it that that's 'all she wrote.' We've got the synthetic theory of evolution.

Unfortunately since he made those statements for the New York Education Department Dr. Eldredge has changed his mode of doing science and has now adopted evolution as a "true belief" rather than just an axiom.

It was pointed out that Dobzhansky said that he never knew of a mutation in his fruit flies that would have been beneficial out in nature and Dr. Eldredge replied, "That weren't lethal. People in America and the world often think that scientists have a bunch of answers. It's a difficult thing. It's a view that is not good." He said that the problem with neo-Darwinism was not so much that it was wrong, but it had some real problems with falsifiability in some of its concepts. Natural selection was particularly hard to deal with except in carefully controlled laboratory conditions. He thought the problem was that natural selection did not explain the diversity of life, so the idea of punctuated equilibria had been devised in an attempt to fill the gaps. The theory said there were differential rates of origination of new species and of their survival. He admitted that punctuated equilibria was still very "evolutionary," and arguments about mechanisms were still going on within the evolutionary camp.

In his 1980 book, Douglas Hofstadter addressed the mind-boggling problem of the origin of life by a mechanistic process:

> "A natural and fundamental question to ask on learning of these incredibly interlocking pieces of

software and hardware is: 'How did they ever get started in the first place?' It is truly a baffling thing. One has to imagine some sort of bootstrap process occurring, somewhat like that which is used in the development of new computer languages — but a bootstrap from simple molecules to entire cells is almost beyond one's power to imagine. There are various theories on the origin of life. They all run aground on this most central of all central questions: 'How did the Genetic Code, along with the mechanisms for its translation (ribosomes and RNA molecules), originate?' For the moment, we will have to content ourselves with a sense of wonder and awe, rather than with an answer.'"[26]

Leslie Orgel wrote in the 15 April 1982 issue of *New Scientist* about the gigantic problem of the origin of life: "We do not yet understand even the general features of the origin of the genetic code.... The origin of the genetic code is the most baffling aspect of the problem of the origins of life, and a major conceptual or experimental breakthrough may be needed before we can make any substantial progress."[27] In other words, as Dr. Eden said, we must await the discovery of new natural laws because the ones now known to be operating could not permit such an event.

Manfred Eigen of Germany, well-known in this field, often treats the gigantic problems with little concern by making assumptions: "It was therefore necessary for the first organizing principle to be highly selective from the start. It had to tolerate an enormous overburden of small molecules that were biologically 'wrong' but chemically possible.... The primitive soup did face an energy crisis, early life forms needed somehow to extract chemical energy from the molecules in the soup. For the story we have to tell here it is not important how they did so; some system of energy storage and delivery based on phosphates can be assumed."[28] Most critics of evolution theory would be happy to grant Dr. Eigen an energy source and storage if he would just explain *how* nonliving chemicals could become organized in the first place to permit life to begin.

He did restate the problem, but not the solution: "One can safely assume that primordial routes of synthesis and differen-

tiation provided minute concentrations of short sequences of
nucleotides that would be recognized as 'correct' by the
standards of today's biochemistry."[29] The information content
of this sentence is that he assumes that life started spontaneously, and he thinks that it is safe to assume this because he
knows that the scientific community, who should be critically
evaluating such propositions, all accept the materialistic
explanation of the origin of life on a philosophical basis. He
does appreciate the magnitude of the problem, for he said,
"Which came first, function or information? As we shall show,
neither one could precede the other; they had to evolve together."[30] This is the case throughout the assumed evolutionary process. For any new structure to come into existence,
it would have required a host of highly coordinated structures
and functions to originate simultaneously.

Dr. Patterson felt very strongly that no one had yet given a
satisfactory explanation of the origin of the first living cell.
When asked, "How could that have just happened by accident?" He replied unhesitatingly, "It couldn't. Absolutely,
I agree."

Methodology in Science Instruction

There was a mixed but very confusing reaction among the
museum officials about whether school and university students
should be told about the scientific evidence that was contradictory to evolution theory. To the question, should both
sides be taught?, Dr. Patterson said, "No." He said, "How are
you going to bring up a child telling him all the things we
aren't sure about?" When he was asked how it would harm a
student to know these things, he replied that he could not
understand why you should give a young child the facts and
let him choose for himself. This of course makes a lot of sense,
but that is not what is being sought for public education.
Young students should not be taught about complex subjects,
like theories on origins, when there is much debate among
scientists about them. When they become old enough to
evaluate the evidence themselves, then they can be presented
the theories and relevant evidence. The philosophical bias
of the school system or individual teachers should not be

allowed to be used as a basis for indoctrination in a pluralistic society.

After some discussion Dr. Patterson said, "The thing I agree with is the philosophy. I will certainly agree that the first thing you do is what was done in the Middle Ages: take students up through Plato, Aristotle, Socrates and Descartes, etc., to teach them philosophy and how to recognize truth when they find it. If there is no way of recognizing it, tell them that. From then on say, 'All right, we don't have time to tell you all the facts so we'll give you our story. If you can pick holes in it, then by all means do.' " He still had a strong inclination to tell only the establishment side of the story on origins.

Dr. Eldredge asked if the committee studying the question of how the state should teach theories on origins wanted to give equal time for creationism? He was told that since there were only two models on origins, they were trying to evaluate, for instance, whether a book like Wysong's *The Creation/Evolution Controversy* should be placed as a reference book in schools. He replied, "I would like to say this on tape that my feeling about that is that students always should be exposed to the fact that there are at least two, and, as you said, perhaps more. At least in terms of modern intellectual life there are these two basic sets of assumptions about the nature of the living world."

Question: "You don't object to both being taught?" Dr. Eldredge replied, "I don't object. In fact, it should be done. I think that would be good. However, in a course in biology which deals with science, I think the science version should not be presented along side of some other thing which is not science." Which version did he think was science? He thought the basic evolutionary theory, "fraught with error as it is" was science. Imperfect though it might be, he thought it was science, even though he admitted that it was just one of two possible axioms and there was a problem with testability. He said, "For the record this is the area that should be taught in biology, not creationism. I do not wish to be construed as supporting the teaching of both! However, it would be entirely appropriate at the outset to point out that creationism is another whole way of explaining the diversity of life. I also wish, though, basically, that all science would be taught in such a way that it was a normal human inquiry into the natural world. . . ." He thought that the logic was no different than that involved in literary criticism and that there was "nothing sacrosanct about science, there is nothing definite about it or definitive about it." He thought all of America would benefit if science were taught this way.

It was pointed out to Dr. Eldredge that people who defend evolution theory say that it proceeds too slowly over too long a time span to be tested in the laboratory. He replied, "No, you can't test natural selection or anything more than from one generation to another. In the fossil record you are dealing with things that are not subject to that. Needless to say, in the natural world it is hard to get that kind of data. You can't get it from long-dead organisms."

What did Dr. Eldredge think was the most difficult problem for evolution theory? He replied, "Making both aspects of the study of evolution more scientific is the ace number-one problem, probably." He said that there were a number of problems left untouched just in sorting out what was related to what. But as far as macroevolution was concerned, he said that his ''new theory that macroevolution is not reducible to microevolution'' explained it.

Hoyle and Wickramasinghe made an interesting conclusion about whether Darwinism had succeeded in replacing Paley's argument for design:

> The speculations of *The Origin of Species* turned out to be wrong, as we have seen in this chapter. It is ironic that the scientific facts throw Darwin out, but leave William Paley, a figure of fun to the scientific world for more than a century, still in the tournament with a chance of being the ultimate winner.[31]

Indeed in the concluding chapters of their 1981 book, they declared him the winner hands down, for life was in every respect "deliberate." They said, "there are so many flaws in Darwinism that one can wonder why it swept so completely through the scientific world, and why it is still endemic today."[32]

In the *The Bone Peddlers*, William Fix, after documenting how the various assumed ancestors of man had been discredited, then went on to enumerate the difficulties with other aspects of evolution, such as the lack of transitional fossils and the vacuous nature of natural selection. He pointed out that many prominent evolutionists like Ernst Mayr and George Gaylord Simpson had admitted that Darwin really did not solve the question of how the different species originated. He questioned "how in *Cosmos* (1980) Carl Sagan can invoke natural selection as if this were an uncontested and immutable law of nature" when it was pure speculation with no positive evidence that it was ever responsible for creating anything new.[33]

He completely agreed with Norman Macbeth that the public was not being informed about the true status of evolution theory: "More than one responsible person has voiced concern that the real facts about Darwinism and evolution are simply not reaching the public."

Norman Macbeth's Harvard Debate

In a debate sponsored by the humanist chaplain at Harvard University in September 1983 between Norman Macbeth and Dr. Kenneth Miller, Macbeth made the following statement:[34] "Here I should again make it clear that Darwinism and evolution are not the same thing. Evolution is the course of change through time, and Darwinism is the explanation of it. I think that the change in the course of time — the evolution — is beyond challenge. You can see it in the fossils very clearly, and you can almost see it in a few centuries or even a lifetime. Darwinism is a different affair, one of explaining it. My attack in my book and elsewhere was on the ideas of Charles Darwin, explaining the mechanism by which the changes occurred. I am not a professional biologist.... I have got into the ptolemics — the thrusting and parrying back and forth on the problems of Darwinism — and for that you don't need too profound a knowledge of anatomy or physiology.

"I want to make a startling observation that it might be advantageous not to have any courses under your belt in biology. The reason I say this is that as I have dealt with biologists over the last twenty years now, I have found that in a way they are hampered by having too much education. They have been steeped from their childhood in the Darwinian views, and, as a result, it has taken possession of their minds to such an extent that they are almost unable to see many facts that are not in harmony with Darwinism. These facts simply aren't there for them often, and other ones are sort of suppressed or distorted. I'll give you some examples.

"First, and perhaps most important, is the first appearance of fossils. This occurs at a time called the 'Cambrian,' 600 million years ago by the fossil reckoning. The fossils appear at that time in a pretty highly developed form. They don't start very low and evolve bit by bit over long periods of time. In the lowest fossil-bearing strata of all, they are already there and are pretty complicated in more-or-less modern form.

"One example of this is the little animal called the trilobite. There are a great many fossils of the trilobite right there at the beginning with no build-up to it. And, if you examine them closely, you will find that they are not simple animals. They are small, but they have an eye that has been discussed a great deal in recent years — an eye that is simply incredible. It is made up of dozens of little tubes which are all at slightly different angles so that it covers the entire field of vision, with a different tube pointing at each spot on the horizon. But these tubes are all more complicated than that, by far. They have a lens on them that is optically arranged in a very complicated way, and it is bound into another layer that has to be just exactly right for them to see anything. . . . But the more complicated it is, the less likely it is simply to have grown up out of nothing. And this situation has troubled everybody from the beginning — to have everything at the very opening of the drama. The curtain goes up and you have the players on the stage already, entirely in modern costumes.

"The creationists say, 'That is abrupt appearance,' and they hammer away at that. Instead of building up bit by bit, it appears suddenly, and that to them signifies creation. I don't want to argue that, but I admit it is very strange that there is no slow build-up. The evolutionists have strained very hard to find earlier fossils and have had very meager results.

"I find it odd that a leading evolutionist who is also a specialist in trilobites, Niles Eldredge of the American Museum of Natural History, never even mentions these problems of the eye. He has a recent book directed at the creationists called *The Monkey Business*.[35] He has several pages on the trilobite there, but he never mentions this eye which is really the hardest part of the problem. I think he does it because he simply can't see the significance of all these things when he is utterly convinced that there *must* have been a slow build-up, but we just don't have any fossils for it. Maybe the conditions were wrong, or we'll find them later.

"Then also, if you ask evolutionists what is their best case, normally, their answer is 'the case of the peppered moth in England.' This moth has two forms — the white and the black. In ancient times, up to about the 18th century, the white form was more numerous than the black, not overwhelmingly so, but more numerous. The industrial revolution began at that time in England and, bit by bit, the leaves and other vegetation, as well as the buildings, began to turn grimy and black. The white moths then became conspicuous against the black and sooty background, and they began to be picked off by predators — birds, maybe. It's turning the other way now, and the black forms are getting a little closer to equality again in numbers. This is presented in practically every textbook on Darwinism as a wonderful example of natural selection at work in evolution. But is it anything like that? If you aren't pervaded with the idea to begin with — if you aren't what is now called, 'theory laden' — does that mean anything? There were two forms; there always were two forms and still are two forms. Under certain conditions, the blacks do better; and, under other conditions, the whites do better. But there is no evolution — there's no change. There's no new form, and yet this is presented as their greatest example of what can be done.

"I want also to point out something that I honestly think they are fully aware of. That is the scantiness of their performance over the last 120 years. Darwin's book *The Origin of Species* came out in 1859 propounding the idea of natural selection. The whole point of it was that we would now be able to explain where the animals and plants came from — how they built up to their present form. So, naturally, the first thing you expect is that now we'll have some family trees, some pedigrees, showing how the present moose developed out of earlier forms. A whole series of them should be presented. These are called 'phylogenies' by the biologists. A pedigree is the same thing and a family tree is the same thing. If you look at modern textbooks, you'll find very few family trees. In the early days — in the last century — they had enormous family trees reaching all the way from vertebrates back to the amoeba. All stages were represented in very fancy and complete trees. You hardly ever find anything like that anymore — an occasional bush that is by no means convincing or impressive. The reason why is that they can't trace the ancestry.

"After 120 years, it is possible to say with considerable certainty that they haven't got a single solid reliable phylogeny. And after 120 years, that is a very poor performance. I think they should candidly face up to that and recognize that Darwinism hasn't been producing much."

Macbeth's debate opponent, Dr. Miller, made no attempt to address these specific points. Instead he talked about what he would have said if he had been debating a creationist, i.e., attack a straightforward interpretation of the Bible.

Darwin's Enigma Becomes a Light at the End of the Tunnel

Having made an extensive study of the literature and discussed the scientific evidence on origins with natural history museum officials and geology professors, how would the author summarize the results? Does the scientific evidence point to an answer to the "mystery of mysteries" which so greatly concerned Darwin and every thinking person who has ever lived?

First, because of the traps in which those who have gone before us have become ensnared, a prudent person should exercise a certain restraint about the temptation to assume that science is capable of providing absolute answers to the question of origins. It is incumbent upon any person dealing with metaphysics to never forget these two principles:

- Using purely scientific techniques, it is impossible for us to evaluate theories about pre-recorded history with the same degree of confidence that theories on currently operating processes can be studied.
- Science never absolutely proves any theory; it only disproves some theories and raises our confidence in those that have never flunked a valid test in their most mature form.

This is not meant to be a "cop-out" used to evade the subject, following what has been a rather dismal report on the status of Darwinian evolution theory. It simply must be emphasized that persons who expound on theories on origins are not being forthright if they do not incorporate these principles into their appraisal of the evidence. If textbook authors today were to use these as guidelines in presenting material relative to origins theories, there would be little basis for the hue and cry being raised across the United States and many other free-world countries about its treatment by public education.

Of course, it is easy to enumerate the ideas that have been falsified. This practice is often criticized as being only negativism. But it must be remembered that, since falsification of wrong concepts is an essential part of our gaining knowledge through scientific research, it is most appropriate to discuss the failures along with the successes.

At the outset, to begin on a positive note, it can be stated emphatically that there is universal agreement among Twentieth Century scientists that much change is going on among populations of living organisms and that there is fossil evidence of similar change in the past. Scientists who are creationists emphasize this. The only dispute is over the extent and direction of this change.

Those who use the common-ancestry evolutionary hypothesis as their interpretive framework contend that, although extremely rare, it is possible for the change in organisms to be in the direction of increased complexity, more genetic information content, and more benefit to the organism in its struggle for existence. They postulate that, if insensibly minute increases in order can be amplified by a factor representing billions of reproduction events, then even the complexity of the human brain can be accounted for by a purely naturalistic process. Critics of this view point out that observable change in living organisms is quite restricted and obeys testable principles of genetics.

A wide range of variation occurs in any population with a normal bell-shaped distribution for almost every characteristic, although there are exceptions with certain well-fixed features, like the number of limbs and eyes. As the environment changes, one portion of the population may be more apt to survive than others. The changes in populations, whether due to damages to the DNA in reproduction or the normal intermixing of genes, are all purely random. Changes in populations are thus due to the preservation of those individuals which, by chance, were born with the right characteristics, at the right time, and in the right place to survive long enough to reproduce. This variation and survival process can be called "natural selection," but it never has been observed to create significantly higher levels of organization and intelligence in the DNA.

Just because an organism is able to reproduce and survive in a given environment, what is called "adapted," does not tell us how it adapted in the first place. An organism not suited to survive would have died, but that does not automatically indicate that the ones that have survived got their organs, structures, and functions all by evolution.

There has never been a case established where a living organism was observed to change into a basically different organism with different structures. No observed mutation has ever been demonstrated to be more beneficial to the overall population out in nature. The genetic machinery is so extremely complicated, interrelated and coordinated that a random change due to a copying error in DNA has been shown statistically to have only deleterious effects within the time restraints that have been considered for the age of the universe. Even if life had existed for an infinite amount of time, there is no known observable process that could increase the level of information significantly in a natural system.

Every system in the universe appears to be eventually

running down, going to a more random state. It takes very special conditions to temporarily reverse this natural tendency towards disorder: an energy supply, an energy conversion system and a blueprint or program consisting of pre-existing intelligence to direct the process. These could not all have been present in a vacuum or on a primordial Earth before there was any life present. There would have been plenty of energy but no conversion system or program to direct it. Energy alone is highly destructive, and it drives any system toward disorder.

If those who believe in evolution are going to make a case for their theory, they are obligated to first demonstrate that some natural process exists that can create order out of disorder. And they must also demonstrate with direct fossil evidence that such a process actually created the diversity of life existing in the biosphere.

Specialists in the world's greatest museums, who are in a position to know the nature of the fossil evidence, although expressing a strong desire to see the theory of evolution validated, have not produced any actual intermediate forms that would indicate the common ancestry of all life. There is not a single example of a series of fossils that would indicate that one form of organism changed gradually into a basically different type with new organs and structures. The lowest rocks that contain indisputable fossils show the abrupt appearance of all major groups of living organisms with nothing preceding them that could reasonably be argued as evidence for an ancestor.

Not only is there a complete lack of fossil evidence to indicate how the first life originated, but no one has yet shown how the enormous amount of genetic intelligence in a single-celled organism could have come spontaneously from non-living chemicals. The state-of-the-art in science and mathematics has advanced to the point where we can now write mathematical models that quite accurately describe real testable natural processes. But evolutionists have been unable to define mathematically a random process that would generate anything approaching the information content of a living cell. Even if 50 percent of all mutations were beneficial, the evolutionary process would not move in a direction of upward complexity, and there is great dispute over whether any observed mutations can be demonstrated to produce more viable organisms out in nature. Everyone agrees that no more than one in a thousand or one in a million mutations are beneficial.

The origin-of-life experiments that have produced a few amino acids have given no indication whatsoever of how DNA or RNA could have originated spontaneously from nonlife. Furthermore, the early-atmosphere conditions simulated have been found to be unrealistic, for it is now generally agreed that evidence in the Precambrian rocks shows that there was free oxygen present which would destroy the products of these experiments. Francis Crick's suggestion that at least the first living cell must have been transported to Earth in a rocketship and Fred Hoyle's contention that random processes could not form even one of the necessary 2,000 enzymes for life are especially devastating to the theory that life arose in a purely mechanistic manner.

The scientific evidence shows that whenever any basically different type of life first appeared on Earth, all the way from single-celled protozoa to man, it was complete and its organs and structures were complete and fully functional. The inescapable deduction to be drawn from this fact is that there was some sort of pre-existing intelligence before life first appeared on Earth. Whether that intelligence was another civilization on some other planet or a supernatural power, science at the moment cannot determine. One thing is certain, if there is life elsewhere in the universe, man does not have any direct scientific evidence of it. There is not even any substantive evidence that planets exist around any star except our sun, regardless of the speculations emanating from many scientists.

Much weight is usually given to the assumption that the fossil record looks like the familiar picture presented in textbooks, known as the geologic column. The sedimentary rocks are supposed to have been formed by the slow accumulation of sediments over millions of years trapping in them the billions of organisms that then formed fossils. This uniformitarian concept has always been disputed by those who believe the rocks were formed instead by catastrophes. Over the past century the pendulum has swung away from widespread belief in catastrophism to belief in uniformitarianism. Then, in the 1980s, even evolutionists began talking about catastrophism and contending that the major fossil depositions occurred in worldwide catastrophes. Some were suggesting that uniformitarianism should be scrapped completely.

It is widely known that there is no evidence today on the bottom of lakes or seas of any significant contemporary fossil formation going on that even remotely resembles what we find in the sedimentary rocks. This alone falsifies the uniformitarian theory. The sedimentary rocks, therefore, do not show a picture of slow gradual deposition, but one of catastrophes that laid down the organisms and covered them rapidly enough to have prevented decay.

Not only does the evidence show that the fossil-bearing rocks were laid down rapidly, but there are sufficient examples of out-of-order fossils to question the idea that the fossils are arranged in the exact sequence shown in the geologic column. Indeed, there are patterns found in the arrangement of rocks that must be accounted for in any model that attempts to explain geological formations. If models are expected to hold up under serious scrutiny, they should include neither the assumption of gradual fossil deposition over long periods of time nor the assumption that the geologic column arrangement actually exists and has been validated. The column is only a hypothetical arrangement for which there has never been developed a rigorous treatise showing how it has been systematically validated.

A geological fact which is perhaps the greatest problem for those who choose to believe that the geologic column was deposited uniformly over millions of years is the lack of meteoric evidence in all but the surface rocks. This is another well-guarded trade secret that has not leaked out, but knowledgeable geologists will admit it if questioned directly on the subject. In a personal correspondence with the author, a former president of The Geological Society of Britain wrote, "I do not know of any record of meteoritic material back in the stratigraphical column unless you accept Alvarez et al's evidence of iridium levels at the Cretaceous-Tertiary boundary." Many scientists, of course, dispute the contention that the presence of a high amount of iridium at several isolated locations indicates necessarily that it came from a meteor. But even if it is accepted as evidence of a meteor, that leaves billions of years of geologic deposits without evidences of meteors. When we examine the moon and Mars it is obvious that they were subjected to much meteoric bombardment. If the sedimentary rocks were deposited uniformly over a billion years, why do they not contain evidence of meteor strikes including huge craters below the surface? That question deserves a serious answer, but believers in uniformitarianism are notably silent on the matter. There have been some suggestions that several basins like Hudson Bay were the sites of giant meteor strikes, but, if strikes actually occurred there, it must have been before the sedimentary rocks were deposited since the evidence is not distinct.

So, if the theory of macroevolution has been falsified and the geologic column was not deposited by uniform gradualistic processes, what do the fossil and geologic evidences tell us about origins? It is this author's opinion that at least two safe conclusions can be drawn without likelihood of their being refuted. These are:

- A number of different types of living organisms first appeared abruptly on Earth in completely functional form at some unknown times in the past. All life did not have a common ancestor.
- The fossilized organisms were buried rapidly in catastrophic events, some of which were on a worldwide scale.

Furthermore, it appears that greatly different conditions existed in the past, when a tropical-like climate extended to the polar regions. Animals and plants grew to very large sizes. The first fossil-bearing rocks appear to contain mostly sea-bottom creatures. But it is also true that at one place or another, rocks classified in every goelogic period lay directly on rocks that have no fossils in or below them. Due to the common practice among geologists to ignore evidence that does not agree with evolution theory or uniformitarianism, it is difficult for us to obtain an accurate picture of the geologic data.

Perhaps critics will say that these are rather timid conclusions because they do not answer a lot of questions that the uniformitarian evolution theory attempts to answer. This might be true, but we must realize that there are limitations to what science is capable of accomplishing. Just because man has been imbued with great curiosity and has thought of many questions is no reason to conclude that he has already found all the answers. Perhaps there will always be questions that will remain unanswered by science. For those, we will be compelled to look elsewhere for the answers. This does not mean that we should not keep searching out the natural world to learn more about its boundless complexities. Our searching, thus far, has paid great dividends as long as we have adhered to the rules of the game in sifting out the conjectures from theories which are about observable, repeatable, and testable phenomena. Let us not abandon these principles that have served us so well for centuries.

The information presented in this book is not now readily available to public school, college and university students, but it should be presented for open discussion along with the host of material that is now supplied in support of evolution theory. As the natural history museum officials said, there are only two theories on origins and both must be accepted axiomatically. The question that the public must be allowed to decide is: should we permit some person or body to select one of these axioms to be taught exclusively, or should students be presented the evidence relating to origins in an unbiased manner so that every person can decide this important issue without coercion? The decision is yours.

References

Chapter 1
1. Charles Darwin, *The Origin of Species by Means of Natural Selection or the Preservation of Favoured Races in the Struggle for Life*, reprint of 6th Edition (London: John Murray, 1902), pp. 341-342.
2. Richard B. Goldschmidt, *The Material Basis of Evolution* (New Haven: Yale University Press, 1940), p. 390.
3. Stephen Jay Gould, "The Return of Hopeful Monsters," *Natural History*, V. 86, No. 6, June-July 1977, pp. 22-30.
4. David Pilbeam, "Rearrangaing Our Family Tree," *Human Nature*, June 1978, pp. 39-45.
5. David Raup, "Conflicts Between Darwinism and Paleontology," *Bulletin*, Chicago Field Museum of Natural History, V. 50, January 1979, pp. 22-27.
6. Colin Patterson, Personal communication to Luther D. Sunderland on 10 April 1979.
7. Stephen Jay Gould, "Evolutionary Theory and the Rise of American Paleontology," *Syracuse University Geology Contribution 3* (Syracruse: Syracuse University Geology Department, 1974), p. 4.

Chapter 2
1. Bert Thompson, *The History of Evolutionary Thought* (Fort Worth: Star, 1981), pp. 27-30.
2. Richard Leakey and Roger Lewin, *Origins* (New York: E.P. Dutton, 1977), p. 25.
3. Gertrude Himmelfarb, *Darwin and the Darwinian Revolution* (New York: W.W. Norton and Co., 1968), p. 172.
4. Benjamin Farrington, *What Darwin Really Said* (New York: Schocken Books, 1982), pp. 110-111.

5. William Paley, *Natural Theology, or Evidences of the Existence and Attributes of the Deity Collected from the Appearances of Nature*, 1st Edition (London: Tegg, 1802).

6. Farrington, p. 19.

7. Stephen Jay Gould, "Darwinism and the Expansion of Evolutionary Theory," *Science*, V. 216, 23 April 1982, p. 386.

8. Edward Blyth, Articles published in *British Magazine of Natural History*, 1835, 1837.

9. Malcolm Bowden, *The Rise of the Evolution Fraud*, (San Diego, CA: Master Books, 1982), p. 4.

10. Charles Darwin, *The Autobiography of Charles Darwin*, 1809-1882, Appendix and Notes by Granddaughter Nora Barlow (New York: Harcourt, Brace and Co., 1958), p. 44.

11. Ibid., p. 45.

12. Ibid., p. 27.

13. Ibid., p. 28.

14. Ibid., p. 52.

15. Ibid., p. 57.

16. Ibid., p. 58.

17. Ibid., p. 60.

18. Ibid., p. 63.

19. Francis Darwin, Editor, *The Life and Letters of Charles Darwin* (New York: D. Appleton and Co., 1898), pp. 277-278.

20. Christopher Rallings, *The Voyage of Charles Darwin* (from PBS series) (New York: Mayflower Books, 1979), pp. 161-163.

21. Herbert Spencer, "Theory of Population," Pamphlet, London, 1852.

22. Ibid.

23. Thompson, p. 64.

24. Ibid., p. 69.

25. Ibid., pp. 71-72.

26. Himmelfarb, p. 240.

27. Francis Bacon, *Novum Organum*, Edited by Joseph Devey (London: Henry G. Bohn, 1853).

28. Beverly Halstead, "Popper: Good Philosophy, Bad Science?", *New Scientist*, V. 87, No. 1210, 17 July 1980,

pp. 215-217.
29. Ibid.
30. Colin Patterson, *Evolution* (London: British Museum (Natural History), 1978), pp. 145-146.
31. R.L. Wysong, *The Creation-Evolution Controversy* (Midland, MI: Inquiry Press, 1976), p. 31.
32. Karl Popper, *Unended Quest* (Glasgow: Fontana Books of Collins, Sons and Co. Ltd., 1976).
33. Halstead, pp. 215-217.
34. Karl Popper, Letters — "Evolution," *New Scientist*, V. 87, No. 1215, 21 August 1980, p. 611.
35. Neal C. Gillespie, *Charles Darwin and the Problem of Creation* (Chicago: The University of Chicago Press, 1979), p. 75.
36. L.H. Matthews, "Introduction" to *The Origin of Species* by Charles Darwin (London: J.M. Dent and Sons, Ltd., 1971), pp. X, XI.
37. Arthur Koestler, *Janus: A Summing Up* (New York: Vintage Books, 1978), p. 185.
38. P.S. Moorehead, and M.M. Kaplan, Eds., *Mathematical Challenges to the Neo-Darwinian Interpretation of Evolution*, The Wistar Institute Symposium Monograph No. 5 (Philadelphia: Wistar Institute Press, 1967), pp. 13, 14.
39. Norman Macbeth, *Darwin Retried* (Boston: Gambit, 1971).
40. Norman Macbeth, "What's Wrong with Darwinism?," Personal interview with Luther D. Sunderland, 29 May 1982.
41. Ronald Brady, "Natural Selection and the Criteria by Which a Theory Is Judged," *Systematic Zoology*, V. 28, December 1979, pp. 600-621.
42. Ronald Brady, "Dogma and Doubt," *Biological Journal of the Linnean Society*, V. 17, No. 1, February 1982, pp. 79-96.
43. Gregory Alan Pesely, "The Epistemological Status of Natural Selection," *Laval Theologique et Philosophique*, V. XXXVIII, February 1982, p. 74.
44. Gillespie, p. 6.

Chapter 3
1. Charles Darwin, *The Origin of Species* (London, 1858).
2. Ibid.
3. Preston Cloud, "Pseudofossils: A Plea for Caution," *Geology*, V. 1, No. 3, November 1973, pp. 123-127.
4. Kai Petersen, *Prehistoric Life on Earth* (New York: E.P. Dutton and Co., 1961), p. 56.
5. John Repetski, "A Fish from the Upper Cambrian of North America," *Science*, V. 200, No. 4341, 5 May 1978, pp. 529-531.
6. G.G. Simpson, *The Meaning of Evolution* (New Haven: Yale University Press, 1953), p. 18.
7. T.N. George, *Science Progress*, V. 48, 1960, p. 1.
8. Preston Cloud and Martin Glaessner, "The Ediacarian Period and System: Metazoa Inherit the Earth," *Science*, V. 217, No. 4562, 27 August 1982, pp. 783-792.
9. Stephen Jay Gould, "The Ediacaran Experiment," *Natural History*, V. 93, No. 2, February 1984, pp. 14-23.
10. Nigel Henbest, " 'Oldest Cells' are only weathered crystals," *New Scientist*, V. 92, No. 1275, 15 October 1981, p. 164.
11. Simon Conway Morris and H.B. Whittington, "The Animals of the Burgess Shale," *Scientific American*, V. 241, No. 1, July 1979, pp. 122-133.
12. Odin, Gale, Auvray, Bielski, Dore, Lancelot and Pasteels, "Numerical Dating of Pre-Cambrian/Cambrian Boundary," *Nature*, V. 301, 6 January 1983, pp. 21-23.
13. Chryl Simon, "In with the Older," *Science News*, V. 123, 7 May 1983, pp. 300-301.
14. Chris Peat and Will Diver, "First Signs of Life on Earth," *New Scientist*, V. 99, 16 September 1983, pp. 776-781.
15. Farrington, *What Darwin Really Said*, pp. 48-49.
16. Charles Darwin, *The Origin of Species* (New York: Mentor: 1958), p. 309.
17. Francis Crick, *Life Itself* (New York: Simon and Schuster, 1981), p. 79.
18. Ibid., pp. 87-88.
19. Ibid., pp. 117-141.
20. John Gribbin, "Carbon Dioxide, Ammonia — and Life,"

New Scientist, V. 94, NO. 1305, 13 May 82, pp. 413-416.

21. Monitor, "Smaller planets began with oxidised atmospheres," *New Scientist,* V. 87, No. 1209, 10 July 1980, p. 112.

22. Harry Clemmey and Nick Badham, "Oxygen in the Precambrian Atmosphere: An Evaluation of the Geological Evidence," *Geology,* V. 10, March 1982, p. 141.

23. Philip Morrison, "Books," *Scientific American,* V. 250, No. 4, April 1984, pp. 30-31.

24. Gribbin, p. 416.

25. Fred Hoyle and Chandra Wickramasinghe, *Evolution from Space* (London: J.M. Dent and Co., 1981), pp. 141, 144.

26. Ibid., p. 28.

27. Ibid., p. 131.

28. "Hoyle on Evolution," *Nature,* V. 294, 12 November 1981, p. 105.

29. *Encyclopedia Britannica,* "Life on Earth," V. 10, 1974, p. 894.

30. John Maynard Smith, *Evolution Now: A Century After Darwin* (London: The Macmillan Press Ltd., 1982).

31. Stephen Jay Gould, "An Early Start," *Natural History,* V. 87, February 1978.

32. Fred Hoyle, "The Big Bang in Astronomy," *New Scientist,* V. 92, No. 1280, 19 November 1981, pp. 521-27.

33. George Wald, "The Origin of Life," *The Physics and Chemistry of Life* (New York: Simon and Schuster, 1955), p. 12.

34. Carl Sagan, "COSMOS," Produced by Greg Andorfer, Broadcast on PBS, September-December 1980.

35. A.S. Romer, *Vertebrate Paleontology,* 3rd Edition (Chicago: University of Chicago Press, 1966).

36. Gould, "The Return of the Hopeful Monsters," *Natural History,* V. 86, June-July 1977, pp. 22-30.

Chapter 4

1. Colin Patterson, Personal communication to L.D. Sunderland, 10 April 1979.

2. Alan Feduccia and Harrison Tordoff, "Feathers of

Archaeopteryx: Asymmetric Vanes Indicate Aero-dynamic Function," *Science*, V. 203, No. 4384, 9 March 1979, pp. 1021-1022.

3. John Ostrom, "Bird Flight: How Did It Begin?", *American Scientist*, V. 67, No. 1, January-February 1979, pp. 46-56.

4. Roger Lewin, "How Did Vertebrates Take to the Air?", *Science*, V. 221, No. 4605, 1 July 1983, pp. 38-39.

5. Ibid.

6. Francis Hitching, *The Neck of the Giraffe: Where Darwin Went Wrong* (New Haven, CT: Ticknor and Fields, 1982), pp. 34-36.

7. "Bone Bonanza: Early Bird and Mastodon," *Science News*, V. 112, 2 September 1977, p. 198.

8. John Ostrom, "Origin of Birds," Lecture for MACUB Conference at Iona College, New Rochelle, New York, 5 November 1983.

9. Duane Gish vs. Kenneth Miller, Debate at Tampa, Florida, 1982.

10. "Whales of the World," supplement, *National Geographic*, V. 150, No. 6, December 1976.

11. Colin Patterson, Personal communication to Luther D. Sunderland on 10 April 1979.

12. Gerald Fleischer, *Evolutionary Principles of the Mammalian Middle Ear* (Berlin: Springer-Verlag, 1978).

13. R. Eric Lombard, "Review of Evolutionary Principles of the Mammalian Middle Ear," *Evolution*, V. 33, No. 4, 1980, p. 1230.

14. Tom Kemp, "The Reptiles that Became Mammals," *New Scientist*, V. 92, 4 March 1982, p. 583.

15. G.G. Simpson, *Tempo and Mode in Evolution* (New York: Columbia University Press, 1944), p. 105.

16. Ibid., p. 107.

17. Roger Lewin, "Bones of Mammals' Ancestors Fleshed Out," *Science*, V. 212, 26 June 1981, p. 1492.

18. Gavin DeBeer, *Atlas of Evolution* (London: Nelson, 1964), p. 48, Colour Plate 3: Paleontology: Evolution of the Horses.

19. Bernarr Vance and D.F. Miller, *Biology for You*, 5th

Edition (Philadelphia: Lippincott, 1963), p. 531.
20. N. Heribert-Nilsson, *Synthetische Artbildung* (Gleerup, Sweden: Lund University, 1954).
21. A.S. Romer, *Vertebrate Paleontology*, 3rd Edition (Chicago: University of Chicago Press, 1966).
22. Hitching, p. 30.
23. Niles Eldredge, 20/20 Program, ABC Television, Sylvia Chase Interview, 14 February 1981.
24. William Hill, C.O., *Primates* (Edinburgh: Edinburgh University Press, V. 1, 1953), pp. 25-26.
25. David Pilbeam, "Rearranging Our Family Tree," *Human Events*, June 1978, pp. 39-45.
26. William R. Fix, *The Bone Peddlers* (New York: Macmillan Publishing Company, 1984), pp. 150-153.
27. Ibid., p. 182.
28. Colin Patterson, *Evolution* (London: British Museum (Natural History), 1978).
29. Patterson, Personal communication.
30. Duane T. Gish, *Evolution? The Fossils Say No!* (San Diego: Master Books, 1981), Public School Edition.
31. Wysong, *The Creation-Evolution Controversy* (Midland, Michigan: Inquiry Press, 1976).
32. Neal C. Gillespie, *Charles Darwin and the Problem of Creation* (Chicago: The University of Chicago Press, 1979), p. 75.
33. Ibid., p. 77.
34. E.J.H. Corner, *Contemporary Botanical Thought*, ed. by A.M. MacLeod and L.S. Cobley (Chicago: Quadrangle Books, 1961), p. 97.
35. E.C. Olson, *The Evolution of Life* (New York: The New American Library, 1965), p. 94.
36. Ibid.
37. David Attenborough, *Life on Earth* (London: Collins/BBC, 1979), pp. 310-11.
38. Fred Hoyle and Chandra Wickramasinghe, *Evolution from Space* (London: J.M. Dent and Co., 1981), pp. 81.

Chapter 5
1. Charles Darwin, *The Origin of Species* (New York:

Mentor, 1958), pp. 224-225.

2. Richard B. Goldschmidt, *The Material Basis of Evolution* (New Haven: Yale University Press, 1940), p. 390.

3. Stephen Jay Gould, "Evolution as Fact and Theory," *Discover*, May 1981, p. 36.

4. Ibid., p. 37.

5. George Alexander, "Alternate Theory of Evolution Considered," *Los Angeles Times*, 19 November 1978.

6. David Raup, "The Revolution in Evolution," *World Book Encyclopedia Yearbook*, 1980, pp. 197-209.

7. Macbeth, *Darwin Retried.*

8. Jerry Adler and John Carey, "Is Man a Subtle Accident?," *Newsweek*, 3 November 1980, pp. 95-96.

9. Steven M. Stanley, *Macroevolution: Pattern and Process* (San Francisco: W.H. Freeman and Co., 1979).

10. Steven M. Stanley, "The New Evolution," *Johns Hopkins Magazine*, June 1982, pp. 6-11.

11. Stephen Jay Gould, Lecture at Hobart and William Smith College, "Is a New and General Theory of Evolution Emerging?" 14 February 1980.

12. Theodosius Dobzhansky, *Genetics and the Origin of Species*, 3rd Edition (New York: Columbia University Press, 1951).

13. Simpson, *Tempo and Mode in Evolution* (New York: Columbia University Press, 1944).

14. Miranda Robertson, "Natural Selection," *Nature*, V. 309, 10 May 1984, p. 106.

15. Niles Eldredge and Gould, "Punctuated Equilibria: The Tempo and Mode of Evolution Reconsidered," *Paleobiology*, V. 3, Spring 1977, pp. 145-146.

16. Robert M. Young, "The Darwin Debate," *Marxism Today*, V. 26, April 1982, p. 21.

17. Ernst Mayr and William B. Provine, *The Evolutionary Synthesis* (Cambridge: Harvard University Press, 1980), p. 229.

18. Immanuel Velikovsky, *Worlds in Collision* (New York: Dell Publishing Co., 1950).

19. Immanuel Velikovsky, *Earth in Upheaval* (New York: Dell Publishing Co., 1955).

20. John Maddox, "Extinctions by Catastrophe?," *Nature*, V. 308, 19 April 1984, p. 685.
21. Stephen J. Gould, "Evolution's Erratic Pace," *Natural History*, V. 86, No. 5, April-May 1977, pp. 12-16.
22. Norman Macbeth, "Darwinism: A Time for Funerals — An Interview with Norman Macbeth," *Towards*, Fair Oaks, California, V. 2, Spring 1982.
23. Duane Gish vs. Ashley Montagu, Debate, Princeton University, 12 April 1980.
24. *Encyclopedia Britannica*, "Haeckel," 15th Edition, V. IV, p. 831.
25. Assmusth and Hull, *Haeckel's Frauds and Forgeries* (India: Bombay Press, 1911).
26. G.A. Kerkut, *Implictions of Evolution* (New York: Pergamon Press, 1960), p. 66.
27. Charles Singer, *A History of Biology* (London: Abelard-Schuman, 1931), p. 487.
28. S. Schwabenthan, "Life Before Birth," *Parents*, V. 54, October 1979, pp. 31-40.
29. Gavin DeBeer, *Homology, An Unsolved Problem* (Oxford: Oxford University Press, 1971).
30. William Fix, *The Bone Peddlers*, p. 189.

Chapter 6
1. Stephen Jay Gould, Introduction to *What Darwin Really Said* by Benjamin Farrington (New York: Schocken Books, 1982), p. XIV.
2. P.S. Moorehead and M.M. Kaplan, *Mathematical Challenges to the Neo-Darwinian Interpretation of Evolution*, The Wistar Symposium Monograph No. 5 (Philadelphia: Wistar Institute Press, 1967), p. vii.
3. Ibid., p. xi.
4. Ibid., pp. 3-4.
5. Ibid., p. 9.
6. Lecomte du Nouy, *Human Destiny* (New York: Longmans, Green and Co., 1947), p. 34.
7. Moorehead and Kaplan, p. 5.
8. Ibid., pp. 18-19.
9. Ibid., p. 19.

10. Ibid., p. 14.
11. Ibid., p. 17.
12. Ibid., p. 47.
13. Ibid., pp. 50-51.
14. Ibid., p. 54.
15. Ibid., p. 58.
16. Ibid., p. 64.
17. Ibid., p. 67.
18. Ibid., p. 71.
19. Ibid., pp. 74-75.
20. Ibid., p. 75.
21. Ibid., p. 76.
22. Ibid., p. 79.
23. Ibid.
24. Ibid., p. 80.
25. Ibid., pp. 109-110.
26. Douglas Hofstadter, *Godel, Escher, Bach: An Eternal Golden Braid* (New York: Vintage Books, 1980), p. 548.
27. Leslie Orgel, "Darwinism at the Very Beginning of Life," *New Scientist*, V. 94, 15 April 1982, p. 151.
28. Manfred Eigen, Wm. Gardner, Pater Schuster, and Ruthild Winkler-Oswatitsch, "The Origin of Genetic Information," *Scientific American*, V. 244, April 1981, p. 88.
29. Ibid., p. 91.
30. Ibid.
31. Fred Hoyle and Chandra Wickramasinghe, *Evolution from Space*, p. 96.
32. Ibid., p. 133.
33. William R. Fix, *The Bone Peddlers* (New York: Macmillan, 1984), p. 181.
34. Norman Macbeth vs. Kenneth Miller, Harvard University Debate, 24 September 1983.
35. Niles Eldredge, *The Monkey Business* (New York: Washington Square Press, 1982).

Bibliography

Adler, Jerry, and John Carey. "Is Man a Subtle Accident?." *Newsweek*, 3 November 1980.

Alexander, George. "Alternate Theory of Evolution Considered." *Los Angeles Times*, 19 November 1978.

Assmusth and Hull. *Haeckel's Frauds and Forgeries*. India: Bombay Press, 1911.

Attenborough, David. *Life on Earth*. Collins/BBC, 1979.

Bacon, Francis. *Novum Organum*. Edited by Joseph Devey, London: Henry G. Bohn, 1853.

Blyth, Edward. *British Magazine of Natural History. 1835, 1837*.

"Bone Bonanza: Early Bird and Mastodon." Science News, V. 112, 24 September 1977.

Bowden, Malcolm, *The Rise of the Evolution Fraud*. San Diego, CA: Master Books.

Brady, Ronald H. "Dogma and Doubt." *Biological Journal of the Linnean Society*, V. 17, No. 1, February 1982.

Brady, Ronald H. "Natural Selection and the Criteria by Which a Theory Is Judged." *Systematic Zoology*, V. 28, December 1979.

Clark, Robert. *Darwin: Before and After*. London: The Paternoster Press, 1950.

Clemmey, Harry, and Nick Badham. "Oxygen in the Precambrian Atmosphere: An Evaluation of the Geological Evidence." *Geology*, V. 10, March 1982.

Cloud, Preston. "Pseudofossils: A Plea for Caution." *Geology*, V. 1, No. 3, November 1973.

Cloud, Preston, and Martin Glaessner. "The Ediacarian Period and System: Metazoa Inherit the Earth." *Science*, V. 217, No. 4562, 27 August 1982.

Corner, E.J.H. *Contemporary Botanical Thought*. Ed. by A.M. MacLeod and L.S. Cobley. Chicago: Quadrangle Books, 1961.

Crick, Francis. *Life Itself*. New York: Simon and Schuster, 1981.

Darwin, Charles. *The Autobiography of Charles Darwin, 1809-1882*, Appendix and Notes by Granddaughter Nora Barlow. New York: Harcourt, Brace and Co., 1958.

Darwin, Charles. *The Origin of Species by Means of Natural Selection or the Preservation of Favoured Races in the Struggle for Life*. Reprint of 6th Edition, London: John Murray, 1902.

Darwin, Francis, Editor. *The Life and Letters of Charles Darwin*. New York: D. Appleton and Co., 1898.

DeBeer, Gavin. *Atlas of Evolution*. London: Nelson, 1964.

DeBeer, Gavin. *Homology an Unsolved Problem*. Oxford: Oxford University Press, 1971.

Dobzhansky, Theodosius. *Genetics and the Origin of Species*. 3rd Edition, New York: Columbia University Press, 1951.

DuNouy, Lecomte. *Human Destiny*. New York: Longmans, Green and Co., 1947.

Eigen, Manfred, Wm. Gardner, Peter Schuster, and Ruthild Winkler-Oswatitsch. "The Origin of Genetic Information." *Scientific American* V. 244, April 1981.

Eldredge, Niles. *The Monkey Business*. New York: Washington Square Press, 1982.

Eldredge, Niles. 20/20 Program, ABC Television, Sylvia Chase Interview, 14 February 1981.

Eldredge, Niles and Stephen Gould. "Punctuated Equilibria: The Tempo and Mode of Evolution Reconsidered." *Paleobiology*, V. 3, Spring 1977.

Encyclopedia Britannica. "Haeckel." 15th Edition, V. IV.

Encyclopedia Britannica. "Life on Earth." V. 10, 1974.

Farrington, Benjamin. *What Darwin Really Said*. New York: Schocken Books, 1982.

Feduccia, Alan and Harrison Tordoff. "Feathers of Archaeopteryx: Asymmetric Vanes Indicate Aerodynamic Function." *Science*, V. 203, No. 4384, 9 March 1979.

Fix, William R. *The Bone Peddlers*. New York: Macmillan,

1984.

Fleischer, Gerald. *Evolutionary Principles of the Mammalian Middle Ear*. Berlin: Springer-Verlag, 1978.

George, T.N. *Science Progress*. V. 48, 1960.

Gillespie, Neal C. *Charles Darwin and the Problem of Creation*. Chicago: The University of Chicago Press, 1979.

Gish, Duane T. *Evolution? The Fossils Say No!* San Diego: Master Books, 1981, Public School Edition.

Gish-Miller Debate, Tampa, Fl., 1982.

Gish-Montagu Debate, Princeton University, 12 April 1980.

Goldschmidt, Richard B. *The Material Basis of Evolution*. New Haven: Yale University Press, 1940.

Gould, Stephen Jay. "An Early Start." *Natural History*, V. 87, February 1978.

Gould, Stephen Jay. "Darwinism and the Expansion of Evolution Theory." *Science*, V. 216, 23 April 1982.

Gould, Stephen Jay. "Evolutionary Theory and the Rise of American Paleontology." *Syracuse University Geology Contribution 3*, Syracuse: Syracuse University Geology Department, 1974.

Gould, Stephen Jay. "Evolution as Fact and Theory." *Discover*, May 1981.

Gould, Stephen Jay. "Evolution's Erratic Page." *Natural History*, V. 86, No. 5, April-May 1977.

Gould, Stephen Jay. Lecture at Hobart and William Smith College, "Is a New and General Theory of Evolution Emerging?" 14 February 1980.

Gould, Stephen Jay. "The Ediacaran Experiment." *Natural History*, V. 93, No. 2, February 1984.

Gould, Stephen Jay. "The Return of Hopeful Monsters." *Natural History*, V. 86, No. 6, June-July 1977.

Gribbin, John. "Carbon Dioxide, Ammonia — and Life." *New Scientist*, V. 94, No. 1305, 13 May 1982.

Halstead, Beverly. "Popper: Good Philosophy, Bad Science?" *New Scientist*, V. 87, No. 1210, 17 July 1980.

Henbest, Nigel. " 'Oldest Cells' are only weathered crystals." *New Scientist*, V. 92, No. 1275, 15 October 1981.

Heribert-Nilsson, N. *Synthetische Artbildung*. Gleerup, Sweden: Lund University, 1954.

Hill, William, C.O. *Primates*. Edinburgh: Edinburgh University Press, V. 1, 1953.

Himmelfarb, Gertrude. *Darwin and the Darwinian Revolution*. New York: W.W. Norton and Co., 1968.

Hitching, Francis. *The Neck of the Giraffe — Where Darwin Went Wrong*. New Haven, CT: Ticknor and Fields, 1982.

Hofstadter, Douglas. *Godel, Escher, Bach: An Eternal Golden Braid*. New York: Vintage Books, 1980.

Hoyle, Fred. "The Big Bang in Astronomy." *New Scientist*, V. 92, No. 1280, 19 November 1981.

Hoyle, Fred, and Chandra Wickramasinghe. *Evolution from Space*. London: J.M. Dent and Co., 1981.

"Hoyle on Evolution." *Nature*, V. 294, 12 November 1981.

Kemp, Tom. "The Reptiles that Became Mammals." *New Scientist*, V. 92, 4 March 1982.

Kerkut, G.A. *Implications of Evolution*. New York: Pergamon Press, 1960.

Koestler, Arthur. *Janus: A Summing Up*. New York: Vintage Books, 1978.

Leakey, Richard, and Roger Lewin. *Origins*. New York: E.P. Dutton, 1977.

Lewin, Roger. "Bones of Mammals' Ancestors Fleshed Out." *Science*, V. 212, 26 June 1981.

Lewin, Roger. "How Did Vertebrates Take to the Air?" *Science*, V. 221, No. 4605, 1 July 1983.

Lombard, R. Eric. "Review of Evolutionary Principles of the Mammalian Middle Ear." *Evolution*, V. 33, No. 4, 1980.

Macbeth, Norman. *Darwin Retried*. Boston: Gambit, 1971.

Macbeth, Norman. "Darwinism: A Time for Funerals — An Interview with Norman Macbeth." *Towards*, Fair Oaks, CA, V. 2, Spring 1982.

Macbeth, Norman vs. Kenneth Miller. Harvard University Debate, 24 September 1983.

Macbeth, Norman, Personal Interview with Luther D. Sunderland, 29 May 1982.

Maddox, John. "Extinctions by Catastrophe?" *Nature*, V. 308, 19 April 1984.

Matthews, L.H. Introduction to *The Origins of Species* by Charles Darwin. London: J.M. Dent and Sons, Ltd.,

1971.

Mayr, Ernst and William B. Provine. *The Evolutionary Synthesis*. Cambridge: Harvard University Press, 1980.

Monitor, M. "Smaller planets began with oxidized atmospheres." *New Scientist*, V. 87, No. 1209, 10 July 1980.

Moorehead, P.S. and M.M. Kaplan, Eds. *Mathematical Challenges to the Neo-Darwinian Interpretation of Evolution*. The Wistar Institute Symposium Monograph No. 5, Philadelphia: Wistar Institute Press, 1967.

Morris, Simon Conway and H.B. Whittington. "The Animals of the Burgess Shale." *Scientific American*, V. 241, No. 1, July 1979.

Morrison, Philip. "Books." *Scientific American*, V. 250, No. 4, April 1984.

Odin, Gale, Auvray, Bielski, Dore, Lancelot and Pasteels. "Numerical Dating of Pre-Cambrian/Cambrian Boundary." *Nature*, V. 301, 6 January 1983.

Olson, E.C. *The Evolution of Life*. New York: The New American Library, 1965.

Orgel, Leslie. "Darwinism at the Very Beginning of Life." *New Scientist*, V. 94, 15 April 1982.

Ostrom, John. "Bird Flight: How Did It Begin?" *American Scientist*, V. 67, No. 1, January-February 1979.

Ostrom, John. "Origin of Birds." Lecture for MACUB Conference at Iona College, New Rochelle, New York, 5 November 1983.

Paley, William. *Natural Theology, or Evidences of the Existence and Attributes of the Deity Collected from the Appearances of Nature*. London: Tegg, 1802 (1st Edition).

Patterson, Colin. *Evolution*. London: British Museum (Natural History), 1978.

Patterson, Colin. Personal communication to Luther D. Sunderland on 10 April 1979.

Peat, Chris and Will Diver. "First Signs of Life on Earth." *New Scientist*, V. 99, 16 September 1983.

Pesely, Gregory Alan. "The Epistemological Status of Natural Selection." *Laval Theologique et Philosophique*, V. XXXVIII, February 1982.

Petersen, Kai. *Prehistoric Life on Earth.* New York: E.P. Dutton and Co., 1961.

Pilbeam, David. "Rearranging Our Family Tree." *Human Nature*, June 1978.

Popper, Karl. Letters — "Evolution." *New Scientist*, V. 87, No. 1215, 21 August 1980.

Popper, Karl. *Unended Quest.* Glasgow: Fontana Books of Collins, Sons and Co. Ltd., 1976.

Rallings, Christopher. *The Voyage of Charles Darwin* (from PBS series). New York: Mayflower Books, 1979.

Raup, David. "Conflicts Between Darwinism and Paleontology. *Bulletin*, Chicago Field Museum of Natural History, V. 50, January 1979.

Raup, David. "The Revolution in Evolution." *World Book Encyclopedia Yearbook*, 1980, pp. 197-209.

Repetski, John. "A Fish from the Upper Cambrian of North America." *Science*, V. 200, No. 4341, 5 May 1978.

Robertson, Miranda. "Natural Selection." *Nature*, V. 309, 1984.

Romer, A.S. *Vertebrate Paleontology.* 3rd Edition, Chicago: University of Chicago Press, 1966.

Sagan, Carl. "COSMOS." Produced by Greg Andorfer, Broadcast on PBS, September-December 1980.

Schwabenthan, S. "Life Before Birth." *Parents Magazine*, V. 54, October 1979.

Simon, Chryl. "In with the Older." *Science News*, V. 123, 7 May 1983.

Simpson, G.G. *Tempo and Mode in Evolution.* New York: Columbia University Press, 1944.

Simpson, G.G. *The Meaning of Evolution.* New Haven: Yale University Press, 1949.

Singer, Charles. *A History of Biology.* London: Abelard-Schuman, 1931.

Smith, John Maynard. *Evolution Now: A Century After Darwin.* London: The Macmillan Press Ltd., 1982.

Spencer, Herbert. "Theory of Population." Pamphlet, London, 1852.

Stanley, Steven M. *Macroevolution: Pattern and Process.* San Francisco: W.H. Freeman and Co., 1979.

Stanley, Steven M. "The New Evolution." *Johns Hopkins Magazine*, June 1982.

Thompson, Bert. *The History of Evolutionary Thought.* Fort Worth: Star, 1981.

Vance, Bernarr, and D.F. Miller. *Biology for You.* 5th Edition, Philadelphia: Lippincott, 1963.

Velikovsky, Immanuel. *Worlds in Collison.* New York: Dell Publishing Co., 1950.

Velikovsky, Immanuel. *Earth in Upheaval.* New York: Dell Publishing Co., 1955.

Wald, George. "The Origin of Life." *The Physics and Chemistry of Life*, New York: Simon and Schuster, 1955.

"Whales of the World." Supplement, *National Geographic*, V. 150, No. 6, December 1976.

Wysong, R.L. *The Creation-Evolution Controversy.* Midland, Michigan: Inquiry Press, 1976.

Young, Robert M. "The Darwin Debate." *Marxism Today*, V. 26, April 1982.

Author Index

Topical Index

About the Author

LUTHER D. SUNDERLAND, B.S. (Penn State University), an aerospace engineer with the General Electric Company, has been involved for 30 years with the research and development of automatic flight control systems (autopilots) for a number of aircraft such as the F-111, Boeing 757 and 767. He has been elected to the engineering honor society Tau Beta Pi, is an Associate Fellow in the American Institute for Aeronautics and Astronautics, has authored many published articles and papers on aviation, and holds a number of patents in his field. As an avocation he has spent over 20 years intensively studying the scientific evidences relating to theories on origins. He has appeared frequently on radio and television and lectured over 500 times on three continents to civic organizations, state and congressional legislative committees, science teachers organizations and many universities about this topic. He recently assisted the New York State Board of Regents in a study of how theories on origins could legally be taught in public schools. He is author of the audio-visual presentation, "Scientific Evidences on Origins: What Do The Fossils Say?"

906